Her Sister Bella a
By Helg:

Contents

Feodora *3*

A Modern Romeo and Juliet *13*

A Question of Class *20*

Her Sister Bella *31*

The Poetess *57*

Images on my Bedroom Walls *75*

Berlin *93*

My Three Sons *102*

Carers *121*

A Teachers Reunion *128*

'Beware of Intruders!' *133*

The Matchmaker *141*

Her Mother's Tale *147*

Who am I? *149*

Unsolicited Confessions   *155*

The Manicure Case   *161*

The Infant Prodigy   *166*

The Psychotherapists   *171*

Felix   *179*

Acknowledgments to Peter, Denise, Christina and Sandra.

Feodora

Wonders will never cease; it was like finding a needle in a haystack in Hyde Park's 'Winter Wonderland' at the beginning of January 2012, a yearly fair, attracting young and old. Children and adults were spoilt for choice; so many rides, so many booths offering local and continental produce to be consumed in situ or taken away. My daughter piloted me through the milling crowd of weary parents and their over-excited offspring, past numerous Austrian bars reeking of Alpine brew. Her fourteen-year-old son, now an 'A' level student, driven by extraordinary energy enjoyed rides up and down, upside down, circling round on big wheels, daring to sample the most hazardous attractions, while his father watched him anxiously.

Opposite one of the exits, the restaurant by the lake seemed an ideal refuge from the ear-splitting, ubiquitous piped music and hurly-burly of the fair. But I was not the only one eager to relax in a more congenial atmosphere. It was packed. Waiters and waitresses slipped with agility through the narrow passages between tables, precariously balancing dishes on trays.

Surveying the scene, I realized, as so often before, that I was one of the oldest people until I spotted a wheelchair-bound elderly lady in conversation with the young man opposite her.

"May I sit here? My daughter is queuing up to order a meal for me. When I am settled she will rejoin her husband and son."

"You are very welcome," Simon replied with an American accent, "and Mama," he looked affectionately at his grandmother, "is pleased to have the company of her own generation."

Just then his partner, Katrina, came to ask what we would like to drink, including me, a complete stranger.

Feodora (she preferred to be called Feo), and I looked at each other. Both of us smiled knowingly. She had read my thoughts. I, too, had sized her up, and began by speculating, "It seems to me that we have much in common."

"You are right. My guess is that you were born in Central Europe and came to this country as a refugee."

Her grandson was taken aback.

"Mama, what is it with you? Have you a sixth sense that enables you to detect someone's place of birth?"

"There are tell-tale signs; a certain expression, intonation," she explained. "I came to this country from Cologne."

"I was born in Frankfurt on Main many, many years ago. As a fourteen year old my parents sent me to distant relatives in Paris. Before the outbreak of World War II, I was lucky enough to get to London. Now I am nearing my ninetieth birthday. The decades have slipped by at such speed. I just cannot believe that I am THAT ancient."

"You call yourself ancient? Guess my age!"

I looked at her. The face was less lined than mine and was framed in loosely waved, light brown hair. It made her appear younger than me.

"Middle, late seventies."

She laughed heartily.

"I am one hundred and two, young lady. My hearing is not as sharp as it used to be. My eyesight has deteriorated badly. I don't always remember where I have put things," she complained. "Well, that is the price we pay if we live longer. I have not been spared either." In an upbeat tone she continued, "Yet we can be proud that we are still here; survivors in more than one sense."

After that, within the next ten minutes, I had summarised crucial events which had occurred in my long life. She had done likewise. This had not been the kind of interrogation indulged in Jewish circles, rather a voluntary exchange or brief outline of past experiences which had made us what we are.

Katrina returned. By then we had established that both of us were retired language teachers living in Wembley.

"Das ist aber unglaublich! (That is quite unbelievable)", Katrina exclaimed.

"You speak the language like a native German," I complimented her.

"I was brought up in Trier."

Emboldened, I asked, "Why did you left Germany, now a far better place than the rest of Europe."

"I chose to study here, at The Royal Academy of Music in preference to any other institution in my country."

The waitress brought the food. Feo, with a healthy appetite, did justice to portions of highly seasoned pasta and pizza after a bowl of soup, as well as a piece of cake with the coffee. In comparison my fare was frugal: mashed potatoes, a poached egg, almost an invalid's diet.

While everyone was busy eating, my imagination started to roam and winged me to St. Petersburg, capital of Imperial Russia until the end of the Great War. In the Tsar's ballroom I glimpsed a radiant Feodora in a satin gown, bedecked with precious jewels, a sparkling tiara in her hair. She danced with her lover under brightly lit chandeliers, both bewitched by the beguiling music.

"I remember buying chocolate called Feodora," the old lady recalled.
That down-to-earth remark broke the spell. I landed back in the real world.

"Mama, we will be leaving in a couple of days. It's back to work in Mexico with the Associated Press. Katrina has decided to come with me. We ARE an item now. She can always earn a living by giving music lessons."

"Without your cheerful presence it will feel lonely again." Feo murmured.

Much later she told me that the couple had split up. A journalist's life-style may have dashed his partner's dreams of (as she put it), "living happily ever after."

* * *

After our first encounter in 'Winter Wonderland' I visited my old friend several times. Before opening the door she would push back several bolts which were supposed to stop any unauthorized person entering the house. But the timber of the door had rotted away in places; it could be knocked down quite easily.

Inside, the large sitting-room facing the garden was full of the heavy oak furniture brought initially from Germany, when Jews were still allowed to emigrate with their belongings. Photographs of four or five generations of her family, placed in neat rows, were displayed on the sideboard. German classical literature lined the bookshelves on the wall. A round table big enough to accommodate at least ten guests stood near the large window. The easy chairs surrounding it were so deep that it was difficult for a short person to get hold of a cup of tea.

She was proud of her three tea-sets. The 'best', into which she poured out the tea during my first visit, was completely irreplaceable should anything be broken. I held my breath as she balanced the teapot, filled to the brim, when she limped back into the room. I told her that I would rather drink tea out of a number three teacup in the kitchen than see her fall flat on her face.

We reminisced about our youth in Germany. As an infant she had lived through the Great War but she could not really remember how the family coped during those years. Her childhood was uninterrupted by the political upheavals during the Weimar Republic and, as a qualified teacher, she found a job in a private school after the family had moved to England.

She was so lively and intent on imparting her story, pausing every so often to find out how I fared, always stressing, "But you are so young, thirteen years my junior! Your childhood in the thirties must have been blighted by the harsh restrictions imposed on us German Jews."

I always used to take my leave after an hour or so because I noticed how much our conversation tired her, although Feo begged me to stay longer. She stood at the door until I was out of sight and then rested until the carer arrived to cook her meal.

"Day in and day out it's chicken, no change whatsoever in the menu," she grumbled.

The carer stayed with her until nine o'clock the following morning, after giving her a cooked breakfast and preparing a cold lunch, insisting that she was not to make any hot drinks. It worried her that she had to leave a thermos flask with tea or coffee in case the old lady would burn herself when pouring it into a cup.

* * *

On my third or fourth visit the door was opened by an elegant, elderly lady in her early eighties. My friend stood behind her smiling.

"May I introduce Lore, my pupil."

"Lore, like in Lorelei, the famous rock in the River Rhine. You must remember the legend and probably read Heinrich Heine's poem about the siren who sang so sweetly that spell-bound boatmen were swallowed up by the water," explained Lore.

"She was in my class, an eleven year old, bright as a button. And by the time she left school we had become the best of friends."

In the sitting-room I watched 'teacher' and 'pupil'. Feo was dressed in a white open-neck blouse, dark cardigan and navy skirt, just as she used to be when going to face her class. Lore wore beige trousers, matching suede shoes and a purple, loose jumper over her still youthful figure; the short, tinted blond hair styled by an expert.

They remembered the girls from long ago. Feo made jokes about her former colleagues whom she had considered utter bores, in those days being the youngest member of staff. She was so animated that her small face grew crimson and her whole fragile, bent body shook with laughter.

"I enjoyed teaching French literature to the older girls. My favourite writer has always been Victor Hugo, such a prolific poet and dramatist. Don't you agree, Helga?"

Without waiting for an answer, she stood up, straightened her body and, with a bow which made her cough, she recited,

'Lorsque l'enfant paraît, le cercle de la famille
Applaudit à grands cris...'

Lore cut her short.
"Enough already! You will suffocate or have a heart attack, Feo. Be a good girl and sit down."
But she did not obey and launched into funny little anecdotes which made her and me laugh.
With a stern look at me, Lore put an end to the merry-making.
"You are over-excited again, Feo; so this conversation stops now."
"No, I'm not. I'm enjoying myself. You don't mind, Helga, if we resurrect the past?"
"Enough is enough, and now, we will have tea."
This was a complete reversal of roles, with the 'pupil' being in charge.

All of us trooped into the kitchen. Feo insisted that the best china should be used as she unwrapped the Genoa cake; we indulged her.
"You go and relax, my old dear."
Muttering under her breath that no one should order her about in her own house, she hobbled away.
I looked round the kitchen. Every cupboard could only be reached by standing on a stool, in Feo's case a ladder.
"This is ridiculous," I remarked. "Why have her children not adapted everything according to Feo's physical capabilities?"
"She does not allow it, nor does she listen to her family or anyone else who is fond of her. She is a cussed old soul. When no one is watching her she balances precariously on the stool to get what she needs. One day someone will find

9

her lying on the floor."

When Lore and I brought in the tea and the cake the 'pupil' had bought, dear Feo was reading in a loud, mournful voice 'Chanson d'Automne' by Verlaine.

> "Je me souviens
> Des jours anciens
> Et je pleure…"

"It's such a sad poem. He must have felt quite bitter when he wrote this. But we certainly do not cry when we recall the past. We have grown into 'hard nuts'."

"You were supposed to sit quietly like a good girl. And you did climb again on that stool to reach the Oxford Book of French Verse. You behave like an obstinate, naughty child and are asking for trouble. I have a good mind to leave now and never set foot in your house again."

That she might lose her best friend frightened her; she started to cry, a sight which would melt anyone's heart.

"All right, all right! Dry your tears and promise to act your age."

Demurely she drank the tea, her face flushed from the mental and physical exertions to prove to us and to herself that her mind was still alert.

* * *

My daughter and grandson were keen to meet a centenarian after I had described Feo's vivacious persona. Nor did she disappoint them. Immediately, she found common ground with the fourteen year old.

"Just because I am ancient in your eyes, Matthew, does not mean that I have lost interest in educational matters," she assured him.

On the way home they could not get over the fact that someone of her age would keep up-to-date and was able to discuss the merits of all the changes that had taken place since her retirement over forty years ago.

A good friend of mine, also a carer, was very eager to drive me to Feo's to see for herself how such an old person could still be so alive to what was going on around her, indeed in the world. We arranged a day. In order to confirm she had entered the date in her diary, some electronic gadget she kept upstairs in her bedroom and could not be persuaded to have brought down for convenience sake, I rang her to confirm the time the previous day.

"Oh, no, no, no! You must not come. I am busy. Some other people are coming."

"Are you sure?"

"Will you wait a minute while I look at my appointments page upstairs."

I heard her put the receiver down and visualized how she climbed up the stairs with great difficulty. She did not want a stair-lift because "I can manage those few steps quite easily."

After about ten minutes, "Are you still there? I cannot find the page; my carer will ring you when she comes. Goodbye."

The carer phoned. She apologized on behalf of Feo who had mixed up the dates and times. On her arrival she found her client extremely confused and exhausted. She must have gone upstairs again to look at the diary.

* * *

Winter set in and I was unable to walk up the steep road leading to her house. She rang intermittently, always

asking, "When will you come to see me again?"
Then there were no more phone calls and no one answered when I tried to ring her. It was not until an acquaintance of mine (a wheelchair-bound lady whose carer shares a flat with Feo's young woman), informed me that Feo had fallen in her house, had been taken to the local hospital, but after a hip operation had got out of bed, injured herself and had been removed to another hospital with her carer having to stay at her bedside day and night.
Almost a month passed before she was fit enough to be discharged. Her family, fully aware that she should not be on her own, arranged for her carer to be with her full-time, a colleague taking over 'the watch' on her day off.
A couple of weeks later I tried to get in touch with her. The carer answered but could not talk. Feo was in the toilet and unable to do her ablutions unaided. When I phoned again Feo answered straightaway. She recalled my visits. However her sense of hearing had severely deteriorated. The carer to whom she handed the receiver had to act as our intermediary.
"My lady is still very weak. She will never recover her former strength completely, but her zest for living seems boundless," she confided.
What is the quality of her life, unable to fend for herself, being completely dependent on others? I cannot imagine what goes on in that old brain which, on good days, still functions, though at a slower pace. She enjoys our visits, but now, at the age of one hundred and five, her power of concentration is diminished. No longer does she entreat us stay when we get ready to go. How does she occupy herself during waking hours? A friend suggested that only a strong-willed or a self-centred person would want to cope with such an existence!

A modern Romeo and Juliet

They sat together in the launderette, Sylvia, a Romanian, Greek Orthodox girl with Salman, a young Muslim from Iran. Confined in close proximity in the steamy, tiny, windowless backroom, cluttered with striped canvas bags, a small fridge, a television on two boxes in lieu of a table, they greedily consumed greasy pizzas bought at the supermarket across the road.

Weekdays Sylvia worked part-time in a bakery. To increase her income, she had applied to the semi-retired proprietor, Salman's father, to employ her as a trustworthy assistant during Saturday's and Sunday's peak hours when his son was in charge.

She, a short, black-haired, rosy-faced and plump girl, had just turned nineteen. He was lean; his dark eyes betraying his religious and philosophical uncertainties, was two years her senior.

What had attracted him straight away was her sweet smile, sunny disposition, insouciance of problems regarding the neighbourhood's ethnic mix. To him, that was a puzzling mosaic in which he had not yet found a niche. Completely at ease with him, it did not occur to the girl that the fathomless chasm between his and her background was unbridgeable. His faith, dominated by customs and taboos, the importance of regular daily prayers, the manifold duties imposed on daughters, wives and mothers in compliance with an unchallengeable doctrine, was completely alien to her upbringing.

Over a period of almost two years, I witnessed a 'Romeo and Juliet' saga being rolled out in the twenty-first century;

the two lovers eventually being dragged apart by their respective families. Salman was pressurized by his intolerant father. Sylvia's parents tried to persuade her to marry a local boy, before she lost her virginity abroad or was too old to become a bride.

Salman, helpful like his younger brother, who was disconcerted when I had once shaken his Muslim hand, insisted on collecting and returning the laundry in view of my advancing years without any extra charge being added to the cost of a service wash. Sylvia started to deliver the clean linen, once she had been introduced to me.

In time she treated me as a surrogate grandmother, confiding how their love had blossomed and how happy they were in each other's company. Not only weekends, but also early evenings before he had counted the day's takings, they would share their 'vigil' until the last customer had left, on occasions as late as nine o'clock.

Liberated at last, they had to conduct their intimate relationship *al fresco*. Salman lived with his family in a flat across the road. From a window his father spied on them at closing time, forcing the couple to leave separately and to meet up later. Then, they walked arm in arm through the streets or hugged and kissed in the darkest corners of the local park, frightened to be spotted by friends. Neither rain nor cold weather cooled their ardour.

* * *

It all came to a head once Sylvia had returned home and letters arrived daily from London, always written by the same hand. Her parents' suspicion was further aroused when she dashed outside as soon as her mobile rang, although they would not have understood what she was saying. Finally, her mother confronted her.

"You are withholding something from us. Who is sending you all those letters? Who calls you on your mobile at least three times a week?"

At first she tried to prevaricate. Moved by her mother's tears, she produced her boy friend's *cris de coeur* and translated them.

"I miss you so much," and, "without you, my non-stop repetitive routine has become intolerable. Please come back to me soon."

"I love him. I want to be with him, Mummy, like you love Daddy, and…"

Her father had arrived on the scene. His voice was sterner, reminding her how they had cherished her, provided for her, protected and nursed her selflessly through illnesses. She owed it to them to be a dutiful daughter and to stay with them in the house in which she had grown up.

"We have looked after you, my child, for many, sometimes difficult, years," he said, "now it's your turn to be a support to your widowed Grandma, and later to us."

"What about my brother? He is much older than I am. Why has no one ever demanded anything of him? That's very unfair."

"He has his own family now and cannot be expected to help us."

She cried until she fell asleep, feeling completely misunderstood by her nearest and dearest. The following morning, after having packed her bags, she left in a huff, tip-toeing out of the house before her parents had woken up.

* * *

Salman's brother had sworn in the name of Allah he would keep the couple's secret strictly to himself, in spite of disapproving of the relationship. Conscience-stricken, as there seemed to be no end to the *affaire*, he blurted out what went on behind his father's back.

The parent's response was swift and drastic. Immediately he took his eldest to task. "You, my first-born, are entitled to inherit my worldly goods. But if you persist in being in contact with the girl, I will cast you out. My estate will be passed on to your sibling. And these are no idle threats!"

Overwhelmed by his father's outburst, Salman made for the door. He was held back by an iron grip. "Get rid of the infidel," his father thundered, before he let him escape down the stairs.

Beset by conflicting emotions during sleepless nights, the young man battled for weeks, coping with the daily routine like an automaton, while his father wisely bided his time in the certainty that his son would return to the fold. He had made sure that relations and friends would close ranks.

Salman began to fear he would forfeit the love of his family and be ostracized by the religious community. Furthermore, he might lose a well-established business; that probability motivated him to face his responsibilities. He also realized that no wonderful future would be in store for Sylvia and him. It had all been an illusion.

* * *

Refreshed after being spoilt at home, in spite of the last

evening's heated argument with her father, Sylvia made up her mind to get married as soon as possible. She was in no doubt that her parents would relent, even forgive their errant daughter, once a grandchild was born. Immature at this stage of her life, ignorant of the fact that such a union was fraught with insurmountable obstacles, she wanted the best of both worlds. She intended to marry the man of her choice and keep her faith. That is why she rushed to the launderette with her hold-all in one hand and a suitcase in the other, as soon as she arrived back in London. After throwing the door open, she dropped the baggage, ran past all the astonished customers on the benches, who had been watching their clothes dancing rondos in the machines.

Salman sat on a stool at the back, concentrating on the business's weekly accounts. A spreadsheet on the screen of his laptop showed totals of takings and expenses. Absorbed in the calculations, he looked up, bewildered, after she had embraced him from behind.

"I'm back, my darling," she whispered in his ear. "Now we can get married. I have worked it all out. With your wages and mine we can rent a little flat, not in this but a less expensive neighbourhood. We can even save some money and in a year or two start a family."

He felt as if a thunderbolt had hit him. Sylvia's enthusiasm overwhelmed him; he stared at her, utterly confused.

"It's what you want too, my love. Your father will accept me as soon as his grandson has been born. He can educate him to become a good Muslim, as long as no one wants to convert me."

Her unwelcome declaration of intent left him

speechless. Disappointed that her beloved had not taken her in his arms and smothered her with kisses, she shrank away from him.

Outside the private little den, low and high-pitched voices mingled with the whirr of the washing-machines. Inside it, they looked at each other like strangers, as if masks had fallen off their once infatuated faces.

Not getting a sound out of the usually articulate young man, she turned on her heels and marched out of the door. In haste, she covered the short distance to my house.

"What has happened in my absence? Why has he changed so completely?" Answering her own questions, she cried out loud, "It's the old boy, his father! Help me, please!"

The girl was distraught, anxious and angry, all at the same time.

On previous occasions she had confided to me the ups and downs of their *affaire*, to which I had listened patiently without taking sides. I made it clear to her as gently as I could that I would not get involved in matters of passion and family problems.

"A fine friend you are," she shrieked, as she stormed out.

* * *

One evening Salman called, now the new owner of the launderette, as a bearer of good news.

"You have been a friend to me over the years and always empathized with my happy tales as well as woes. That's why I want to let you into my secret. I've met a girl, a Muslim girl, introduced to me last Friday outside the mosque."

His eyes sparkled, as he showed me her photo on his mobile.

"You must think my father has had his way. No, I came to the conclusion that the differences between her and my faith and customs were too fundamental. I wrote a letter to Sylvia, begging her to move on."

Has she done so? So far, I have not found out.

A question of class

Upwardly mobile

The garden party was in full swing. At the back of the red-brick, imposing university building groups of young men and women, wearing their caps and gowns with pride, huddled together in the sunshine on the lawn. They were elated, yet apprehensive about their future. The last care-free vestiges of youth were behind them. They faced the real world: professional training or a post-graduate course, once the festivities were over.

"Don't open your mouth, will you, Samantha."

Frank, a towering middle-aged man in ceremonial uniform, buttons polished and medals gleaming, had hissed into his wife's ear before they got out of their two-door car, dwarfed by limousines in the other parking spaces.

Resigned, her slim figure elegant in the navy-blue shift, a wide-brimmed, lighter blue straw-hat over her silvery, curly hair, hazel eyes alert in her discreetly made-up face, she looked distinguished, as she walked at Frank's side in high-heeled patent-leather shoes. Crocheted gloves, matching the colour of her hat, concealed worn, chapped hands.

Their son, chatting with close friends whom he would keep throughout his life, had positioned himself nearest to a group of good-looking girls. Furtively, he eyed the shortest, a hired gown almost reaching her ankles, whom he had watched over the years in the canteen and students common room. They had only exchanged a few words when they happened to be in close proximity.

Yet, there and then, he made up his mind he would marry her, once he had climbed the career ladder high enough to offer her the kind of home someone of her class would expect.

Frank marched towards him. Making his presence felt, he prised his son away from his peers. His wife followed him meekly, wondering if she might be permitted to embrace their only child without causing offence and being reprimanded by him.
"One day," she had promised herself, even shortly after their honeymoon, "I will stand up to him."

* * *

Frank, although an intelligent young man, had been barred by his working-class background from taking advantage of a higher education not easily available for school leavers like him in the middle of the last century. He was the eldest sibling and was expected to contribute to the family's low income. Opportunities, other than long apprenticeships in a trade, were limited. Since childhood he yearned to widen his horizon away from the narrow streets, houses with outdoor toilets and nosy neighbours who wanted to know everybody's business.

Unintentionally he hurt his parents' feelings; they had always struggled to do their best for the children, when his future was discussed.

"I won't be a worker on the factory floor. Nor would I want my wife to wash other people's dirty linen, like you Mum. I want to better myself whatever it takes," he stated categorically.

Soon after Frank had enlisted in the army, the young soldier stood out as a leader of men. After he had seen active service in South-East Asia, his commanding officer commended him for his courage and bravery on the battlefield. He was awarded medals, promoted to the rank of sergeant major. (The higher ranks were not open to him.) Feverishly he desired to reinvent himself, to be upwardly mobile and to be accepted by members of the middle-class as their equal. Therefore he considered it vital for his aspirations to be accompanied by a decorative wife on ceremonial occasions. Unable to attract a middle-class girl, he settled for Samantha, one of the girls in the neighbourhood, because of her good looks and modest, docile demeanour. He hoped, with his help, she would eventually lose the regional accent and improve her mode of conversation, which was peppered with grammatical mistakes.

Yet his wife, pragmatic and practical, had no such illusions and did not share his ambition of grandeur. She was completely comfortable with her station in society; ill at ease as soon as her husband compelled her to follow his example when in contact with 'our betters', as she sarcastically called them.

Not only had Frank been unable to fashion his wife according to his will, his son, too, refused to follow the route his father had mapped out for him. The youngster's great intellect had been nurtured in an elitist grammar school where classical languages were included in the syllabus. The tall, skinny pupil shunned sports and physical activities in which the others excelled.

Although his mother had done her utmost to cook healthy meals, her low wages together with her husband's sergeant major's army pay were not enough to always provide nourishing meals, so essential for the wellbeing of a growing lad.

Frank had fabricated a scenario in which "my so clever son, definitely officer material," would be enrolled in the most prestigious military academy. Bitterly disappointed, he had to concede that this plan would never be realized. The fact that the boy, who worshipped his father, became a successful and esteemed scientist was of little comfort to him. As a result he treated him in the same imperious manner as he did his wife.

Yet, in spite of his erstwhile behaviour towards his family, Frank was endowed with the capacity to love unreservedly. This deep affection was directed towards the grandson on whom he doted, although the boy showed no inclination to become a sportsman or a soldier. In time, Frank, the once obdurate, proud sergeant-major, having mellowed with age, began to approve of his selfless, devoted wife and his ever-supportive son.

Downwardly mobile

Christina's mother opened the door of the three-storey house in a South German town. It was the first time Hannah and Gerald had met Frau Schmidt. Danielle, their daughter, had been a frequent guest during and after the girls' student days. Only German was spoken by the older members of her family; their daughter found little difficulty in making herself understood, considering the few months she had spent in Germany. It had been the easiest time during the four-year language degree course at one of the best English universities.

Entering the lounge at noon, they were deafened by strokes of the grandfather clock near the door and the cuckooing of multi-coloured cuckoos, which popped out of the tiny windows of wooden chalets. All of them were displayed on a long marble-topped sideboard in the tastefully furnished room.

"Lukas's prize-possessions are those clocks, bought from craftsmen in Austria and Switzerland on many holidays," his mother said admiring the collection.

"It is his responsibility to wind them up and dust them regularly. During our holidays Agnes has to do it for him."

Their eyes wandered through the room.

"Surely the hourly bird calls, chimes, cuckooing and strokes of the clocks must disturb you in your sleep?" Hannah observed.

"One gets used to it; actually the walls of this house are very thick."

They stepped through the open glass sliding-door into the garden. The maid's husband, Tomasz, was mowing the lawn. In the pond ducks were fighting over tiny morsels of bread Lukas had thrown in.

The fifteen year old met us with, "The pigeons have pooed all over David again," and giggled.

"This is no way to welcome our visitors," his mother reprimanded him.

Tomasz stopped the mower's motor, drained the pond in the middle of the garden. With a soft, soapy cloth, he carefully cleaned the bronze reproduction of Michaelangelo's sculpture. It was then that Hannah noticed the small lizard, a thin red lead tied loosely round his neck, resting alongside the boy's right foot.

"This is Professor *Bärtchen*, Beardie in English, my pet. He shares my room; he has grown enormously since my parents bought him for me. He likes to go for a short walk when it is not too hot. He eats crickets, live ones. It's a messy job to clean his cage. In winter he hibernates on a tree branch and his messy…"

Frau Schmidt's admonishing glance interrupted him mid-sentence.

Shortly before one o'clock Herr Schmidt, a lawyer, came back for lunch. He shook Gerald's and Hannah's hands having freed himself from his son's bear-hug.

"Where is our beloved daughter? Late again! She knows I have little more than an hour to spare for lunch."

They all stepped through the vast lounge into the dining-room to the sonic accompaniment of the clocks. Agata was ready to dish out the steaming tomato soup; not the variety sold in tins, but home-made with herbs and tomatoes, grown in the vegetable patch in the garden.

When she had returned to the kitchen, their hostess told them, "She is a good cook and manages to keep the house tidy with the help of a local woman who comes in daily for a few hours. She and her husband live in the attic flat: two rooms, bathroom, toilet and small kitchen. They appreciate their comfortable home. We would not invade their privacy during their time off, unless there was an emergency."

"They are not German; I seem to detect a slight accent," Hannah observed.

"Both are Polish. The prospects for young people willing to work hard are so much better here. They are excellent employees, use their own initiative and can be safely left to look after our property during our absence."

Agata cleared away the soup bowls to dish up the main

course: *Wiener Schnitzel,* asparagus (also not out of a tin), bathed in butter and baked potatoes; a feast, according to the visitors.

The girls flew in. Christina apologized profusely.

"I just could not make up my mind which blouse, the pale blue or the turquoise, both satin, would be most suitable with my black full-length velvet skirt. I need to look stunning for our reunion party. Danielle has been most persuasive in advising me to choose the blue."

Lukas made a grimace.

"Stupid girls' talk," he mumbled and speared two stems of asparagus which he piloted adroitly into his mouth.

"You know the Schmidts are descended from a long line of aristocrats," Danielle announced when the family was back in the hotel. "Some of their forefathers were courtiers in the Court of Friedrich I, King of Prussia, after his coronation in1701; later in the Court of the Kaisers until the end of the Great War."

Her parents were duly impressed.

"One would not suspect that at all. They do not indulge in airs and graces, even when dealing with their servants," commented her father.

"I expect Christina's parents are hoping she will marry into an upper-crust family. They have a large circle of friends, among them a few eligible candidates," said Danielle. "But I do not think my friend is ready to settle down. By the way, nor am I."

* * *

Two years later Danielle and her parents were invited to

Christina's wedding. After the church service, the guests were driven in white limousines to the botanical garden. In the airy, oblong restaurant opposite the entrance, facing circular flowerbeds, the *maître d'hôte* welcomed the guests. Waitresses and waiters helped them to find their places at the long tables; the bridal couple and their families were already seated at the high table.

Although they had been guests at other weddings, never before had Gerald and Hannah encountered the scene which unfolded in front of their eyes; the social status of the bride's relatives was poles apart from that of the bridegroom's. The uncouth behaviour of Werner's younger siblings, his mother's ample body packed into a tight-fitting floral dress, his father's obvious discomfort in his only and 'best' black suit with his neck seemingly strangled by a red tie, were proof of his family's working-class background. It was embarrassing to see how they struggled with crystal wine glasses, the array of different forks and knives used for the many dishes of the extensive menu; how his parents tried to silence their over-excited younger children who devoured the food in clumsy haste; their coarse accents intermittently drowned the polite conversations of the other guests.

"How on earth did they meet?" Hannah whispered into her daughter's ear on their way to the ladies room.

"When she had nothing better to do, Christina used to attend all sorts of lectures and meetings on campus. Werner, an expert on a new feat of engineering, had been invited by one of the professors. He spotted her in the audience and later approached her. The bright, attractive, young woman impressed him; so did the questions she put to him and, above all, her social ease.

"Christina was struck by his intellect, seriousness and by the fact that he was completely different from all the young men she knew. They now seemed to her, as she explained to me, 'light weight', while Werner was 'solid'. In short, she fell head over heels in love with him, although he is nine years older."

"Wasn't she worried about how her parents would get on with him and his family?"

"No, not at all. They will be living in Zürich where he has a good job with an engineering firm; so there will be little contact."

"But surely, he will not be able to keep her in the style she is accustomed to, unless she too finds work," her father said afterwards.

"Work: no way will she work. Werner is still old-fashioned enough to insist that his wife does not work; anyhow they both want children."

* * *

The following summer Danielle and her parents spent their holidays in a mountain resort not far from Zürich. They met Christina again; she carried her new-born in her arms in the top flat of an apartment block.

"You must forgive the state the place is in. Baby Hans is forever hungry; so far I have not got into a routine. But I am delighted to see you. Come and sit on the balcony. The university is high above at the back in one of the hilly streets of the town.

You hold Hans, Danielle; I will make some coffee and bring the chocolate cake I managed to bake to celebrate this special occasion."

Both vanished into the kitchen, from where her parents

could hear peals of laughter.

"I haven't laughed so much since I came here," she said as she brought the cake; her friend following closely behind, pushing a trolley with plates and cups.

Christina, cradling Hans in her arms, sat down; Danielle squeezed round her parents on the narrow balcony which wound round the flat's outer wall. She served the food and drink.

"How carefree we were, all of us," her friend reminisced. "We had no worries and were fancy-free, except for getting by with the minimum of work to pass Finals."

Her face lit up with a smile, followed by a deep sigh.

"You, Danielle, are biding your time till Mr. Right appears on the scene, still being cosseted by your indulgent parents. I could not wait to get away from Mr. Wiseacre Lukas (he is really quite a brilliant student), and away from my mother, anxious to marry me off to a young man in her circle of friends. So I practically fell into the arms of the first serious man who showed an interest in me. He was completely different from anyone I had ever met before."

She hesitated for a few moments.

"How can I explain it, even to myself? I had not come into close contact socially with anyone from the working-class. My brother mixes well; he mocks me for being 'stuck-up'."

"To put it bluntly, you did marry a working-class boy, I mean man," their tactless daughter corrected herself.

"It was a challenge. You remember how much I always loved to overcome challenges, Danielle? Though, of course, choosing a husband is a serious matter."

Hannah's daughter nodded. She wisely refrained from reminding her friend of the many instances when things went wrong.

As if reading her mind, Christina continued, "Ah well, it did not always work out. I think I learnt a lot by making mistakes."

Hannah broke the silence which followed.

"You seem happy and fulfilled in the new life and surroundings your husband has created for you. After all, an unlimited amount of money is not a recipe for happiness."

"Werner, you cannot fault him, is a wonderful husband and father. He can do everything: housework, DIY. You name it, he can do it! My parents are experts at delegating everything to paid servants," and, after a little pause, "how I hate that word now, which before had identified someone who was hired to work. Upper, lower, middle, lower middle-class: the class system is just an artificial barrier to put the 'lower orders' in their place! Only since I have been married, have I really grown up."

"Into a little ideological communist, possibly like her husband," Hannah speculated, as the young mother carried on telling them, "With hindsight, I realize how frivolous I have been."

Shortly before Hans was ready for his next breast feed, the family left. Christina had certainly matured into womanhood; they just wondered whether her husband's guidance and influence had undermined her individuality. She had said very little about the relationship with her in-laws, whom she saw at rare intervals. Gradually the bond between the two student friends loosened; each one following her destiny. Eventually, not even Christmas cards with news updates were exchanged any more.

Her sister Bella

Introduction

After Hitler came to power in Germany in 1933 many Jewish families left their homes in the hope of starting a new life in England. Some of the women, even ladies of leisure, had enrolled in dressmaking or cookery classes which would help them to earn a living in the new country, once their savings had been spent. Charities and welfare organizations, admiring their courage, assisted them until they had found their feet.

Others had been even more enterprising by investing their funds in renting or buying large properties in NW6 (West Hampstead) and NW3 (Hampstead) which they turned into boarding houses for fellow-refugees. My landlord in NW6 had come from Berlin; my friend's, in NW3, from Breslau. Both of us were their youngest tenants.

* * *

Bella and Agnes, middle-aged German Jewish sisters from Berlin, arrived in England three years before World War II. Most of their possessions had been left behind; except a few items they could not bear to part with and clothes, packed in two large suitcases, as well as their savings which had been exchanged into English currency.

Sitting in their small rented room in London, they discussed the various options open to them to earn a living.

"The choices we have are two-fold," said Agnes, aged fifty-six, twelve years older than her sibling. "You can make dresses; I can help you with sewing seams by hand

and, don't forget, I am a good cook. Let's make use of our talents."

With a letter of introduction from their synagogue's Rabbi (who had also found sanctuary in England and had known them for years), they were received by an adviser at a Jewish refugee charity. The sisters had decided to wear their best garments, designed and made up by Bella. All the ladies in the building admired them. Thanks to their recommendations, Bella started a dress-making business with a second-hand sewing machine donated to them.

"We cannot remain forever in this place with finished and unfinished dresses hanging on a stand and the double bed taking up most of the room. We are suffocating in here, the two of us. We have made enough money to find a flat," suggested Agnes.

"Not a flat. Think big; we will rent a house and take in boarders. Our boarding-house will be different from all the others owned by Jewish refugees in this area. It will be similar to a continental *pension* or a better-class hotel," was Bella's immediate response.

"You are naïve, my dear little sister. A deposit and references are needed, quite apart from paying a much larger weekly or monthly rent."

The younger sibling was determined to follow through the idea which had come into her head.

"References, what about the Jewish charity? They will oblige and might even lend us some money. As we now have many satisfied clients and more work in hand, the members of the charity will be gratified and count it as THEIR success."

Agnes looked at her incredulously, wondering how their mother's over- indulged, fun-seeking darling could have

out of the blue become such a calculating business woman.
"Even the bank," Bella had not yet finished, "we will make an appointment with the manager. I will use all my charm and will persuade him to arrange an overdraft."
Impressed by the two foreign women's genuine desire to better themselves, the banker made sufficient funds available for their enterprise with affordable interest rates.
In the days that followed Bella went into over-drive, thrilled at being of real use for the first time in her forty-four years. In less than two weeks everything worked out as she had planned. They talked to the local shopkeepers about their new business venture and were offered credit, should they need it.

The estate agent faced the two women whose command of the English language was limited. As soon as he had grasped they wanted to rent a property in the area, he showed them a photograph of a two- storey Victorian house in a quiet street nearby, close to many shops and public transport.
"The owners are letting their house for the duration of the war; the husband is a naval officer, his wife has gone to her family in New York. There is even a possibility that they might sell the house at a later stage, if they decide to settle in America. Do you have time to view the property now?"
They nodded.
He walked with them down the road, took the first turning on the right and stopped at the second house.
"Oh just what we want," Bella cried enthusiastically, even before the entrance door was unlocked.
The sisters were led through double doors into the hall. They inspected all the rooms, the kitchen, the toilet on each

floor and the box room under the slanted roof at the top. "The kitchen will do for the moment. Gradually, everything in the house which we do not like can be replaced," Bella decided without even consulting Agnes.

After the deposit and two months' rent in advance had been paid, they signed the contract.

"What a risk we are taking," wondered Agnes aloud.

"Nonsense! Our first boarder can move in a week's time when the two of us have thoroughly cleaned the place."

"And who might he or she be, may I ask?"

"Ah, that is a surprise."

Bella's face lit up.

"It's a middle-aged woman, slightly mad... No, I mean slightly deranged. I promised her family we would take good care of her when they came here while you were out."

Agnes was horrified.

"It's all above board, big sister, dear. The Jewish charity put me in touch with the family. The lady told me that they have more like her on their waiting list."

"All behind my back!"

Agnes winced, as if she were in pain.

"Does she speak German, Bella?"

"Of course not, they are English Jews. We do not have to speak English to cater for that poor devil's needs. You do remember how I looked after you when you had to undergo surgery a few weeks before our departure? Dr. Bauer told me that I was a good nurse."

Agnes sighed.

"On your head be it!"

The spoilt little sister had come into her own. The business had been launched.

* * *

Had it not been for an unforeseen traffic diversion, Dorothy Talbot would not have driven past the imposing property and noticed the 'FOR SALE' sign fixed to the ironwork gate. Nor would the twin image of the former proprietors, Agnes and her sister Bella, have detached itself from the shadow-land of her subconscious. In all probability with the passage of time, the memory of their world, quite alien to the English, would have dimmed; the vision of their intertwined lives consigned to oblivion.

It all happened over twenty years ago, because Sybil Talbot (a paternal aunt in her late seventies) had reluctantly agreed to sell her flat and had rented a room in a North West London boarding-house.

"You must see my new quarters," Auntie, always positive in accepting the inevitable, had said to her young niece on the phone. "Come tomorrow just before four o'clock and partake in Sunday's tea ritual."

Dorothy's eyes swept over the façade of the property. The hydrangeas, lining the path to the front door, were in full bloom. She grasped the shining brass knocker. It bounced back on the high stained-glass panelled door which was opened by a pert parlour-maid, in a neat black dress and white starched lace-edged apron with bib. She looked at her inquisitively.

"My aunt, Miss Talbot, is expecting me."
"Please come inside."

Dorothy stepped over the threshold into the hall. Nearing the kitchen at the foot of the stairs, her olfactory sense was overwhelmed by a profusion of aromas. A guttural female voice accompanied the clattering, chopping and bashing.

The maid led her upstairs to the first floor. Dorothy's aunt, in a light grey patterned cotton dress, greeted her niece with outstretched arms.

"Tea is being served now, Miss Talbot," reminded the maid.

"Thank you, Mary. We'd better go down at once."

Stopping on the stairs, she pointed to the prints on the wall.

"Mrs Goldmann brought these with her from Germany. They are originals, signed by the artist."

In the spacious wood-panelled lounge, over a dozen elderly men and women were installed round small tables in sea-green upholstered armchairs. Bella poured tea and milk into Rosenthal china cups which she handed to the guests.

"Three lumps of sugar, please, Mrs Bella," said an elderly man.

"No. You are only allowed two, *Herr* Lange. You must follow your doctor's orders," she reminded him.

Dorothy and her aunt found two empty seats; for a few moments they became the centre of attention, not the *pâtisserie* Mary put on each table. Remarks about them were made *sotto voce* in German.

Bella tripped around the room in stiletto heels, leaving a trail of Guerlain's perfume *L'heure bleue* behind her. With eagle eyes she watched the old folk as they helped themselves to pieces of cake.

"What a treat, Mrs Bella."

"Delicious, Mrs Bella."

The old boys and girls guzzled the pieces of cake, quietly wondering why this unusual bonanza had replaced the plain and chocolate biscuits, the usual tea-time offering.

Meanwhile, with an unmistakable air of authority, her sister gravitated towards Dorothy and her aunt.

"When Miss Talbot came to see us, I was not at all sure whether she would be happy here because our guests arrived from Central Europe before the outbreak of hostilities. But when she told me that she had spent some of the inter-war years in Berlin, I thought she would not find the ambience too strange."

Agnes Goldmann's intonation was still un-English, yet she spoke clearly and fluently, as she had attended an English language course. Bella had refused to "go back to school again" at her age, as she knew "all the words" she needed to look after the aged guests. Sitting down at one of the other tables, she sipped tea, daintily raising the little finger of her right hand whenever she lifted the cup to her mouth.

After an hour Mary cleared the tables. The guests slowly withdrew to their rooms; Miss Talbot took her niece upstairs.

"Well, are you reasonably satisfied, Auntie?"

"Yes. I have everything I need, some of my own furniture, including my bed (a special concession), and a bathroom *en suite*. When it is fine, I can sit in the rose garden at the back, read undisturbed or talk to the other residents."

She enumerated further advantages that the move had afforded her.

"Neither Mrs Goldmann, nor her sister, is the average sort of landlady. They themselves had to move into a room in a boarding-house when they first arrived in London; that experience, as well as the trauma of having to leave their home and country, motivates them to provide us with every comfort. I can safely say they are as much devoted to our welfare as to each other. But…"

"There is always a 'but'," Dorothy chimed in.

"Mrs Goldmann is an authoritative lady. Any criticism, however harmless, makes her hackles rise and provokes vociferous outbursts of anger. If her culinary prowess is at stake, she spews fire and brimstone."

"Doesn't that worry you, Auntie?"

"I keep my distance when I see her charge out of the kitchen, infuriated and flushed."

"And the others?"

"They win her over with flattery. Some of the guests lay it on with a trowel; she is most susceptible to that. Real problems we sort out with Bella. In the morning, she flits from room to room after the housemaid, running her finger along the skirting-boards to check for particles of dust. Always elegantly dressed, she never seems to do any real housework; while her sister, in spite of her sixty-nine years, draped in a white overall, sweats over the steaming saucepans like a kitchen hand."

There was a knock at the door. Tony, Mary's husband, a slender young man in a waiter's coat and black trousers, came into the room.

"Mrs Goldmann is inviting your guest for dinner this evening, the first sitting, Madam."

"Please thank Mrs. Goldmann for her kindness, Tony. My niece will certainly be delighted to taste our hostess's delicious food," Miss Talbot replied.

Once they were alone, she added, "The ladies of the house would have been offended, had you refused."

On the dot of seven o'clock the sound of the gong boomed through the house. A dozen guests trooped into the dining-room, dressed in outmoded evening attire. They found their places at the extended dining-table. Ceiling cornices, orchre- tinted wood panelled walls and fine reproductions of old masters gave this room a distinctive character, heightened by an oil portrait of Bella, radiant in all her youthful glory. It hung over the mantelpiece. Two valuable Chinese vases, a gift from one of the guests' sons, stood on either side.

The older sister, having just put the final touches to the meal, had only managed to take off her overall and pat down ruffled strands of grey hair. She dropped her tired, heavy body into the chair, the only one with armrests.

Bella appeared, made up to the nines. Dyed short black hair framed her pale face. Still overpoweringly perfumed, she wore a clinging silver-*lamé* suit, partly to impress the visitor, partly to give the outfit one of its rare airings. A diamond watch sparkled on her wrist; rings adorned her fingers. She advanced gingerly. Carefully she lowered herself into a chair next to Mr Levy, treacle-voiced words dripping from her lips.

"You will have me as your neighbour tonight, won't you, dear sir?"

Indifferent to the unsolicited favour, he shrugged his shoulders. As soon as the mistress of the house had picked up the cutlery, the hungry guests tucked into the appetizing, geometrically arranged *hors d'oeuvres* in front of them. After the first course, Tony, formerly a waiter in seaside hotels, who on his first evening had worn tails and white gloves, officiated with great panache, serving vegetables once Mrs Goldmann had dished out generous portions of meat. Silence reigned, except for the scraping of knives and forks on the china plates. Eating demanded the old people's undivided attention for it was a serious business. Dorothy watched them in amazement. "Nothing seems to be very wrong with their digestive systems," she thought.

A wave of his employer's hand prompted Tony, still in attendance near the buffet, to carry the meat and vegetable dishes out.

"No seconds?" cried a shrivelled old lady.

"No seconds," a disappointed murmur circulated round the dining-table, a sub- *voce* protest.

One obstreperous guest, the gentleman on Bella's left, would have none of it. Brandishing his knife like a dagger, his livid, grey lined-face screwed up, he bellowed in a resounding bass voice, "I want more meat," and, like a spoilt child, banged his fists on the table.

The others held their breath; a drama was unfolding in front of their very eyes, a welcome interlude in their dull, daily routine. Was it a revolt in the ranks? Surely, such behaviour was not tolerated in Mrs Goldmann's establishment?

Bella, always intent on keeping up appearances, oozed unwarranted charm over the offender. "Please, Mr Levy, lay down your knife. This is not done in our *pension*."

"I don't pay good money to be taught table manners! I can do as I like."

Nipping any further controversy in the bud, Mrs Goldmann, retorted in an imperious voice, while Bella gently eased the knife out of the irate man's clenched fist, "I do not agree with you on this point, Mr Levy; therefore I ask you to move out. There is no shortage of applicants who want to rent a room in my house."

Chastened, the old boy calmed down; peace reigned again while the last course was being served.

As Dorothy took her leave, the second sitting was still in full swing. Agnes came out of the dining-room to tell her it had been a pleasure to meet her and that she must come again soon.

* * *

Two years later Dorothy's aunt became housebound for several months due to an unfortunate fall on the stairs. She had hurt her right foot, which had to be put into plaster. Eventually it left her with a slight limp. All meals had to be brought to her room; when a nurse was not in attendance Bella undertook to help the invalid to wash and dress, all without extra charge.

Miss Talbot's confidence had been severely undermined by the fall. Dorothy, her only near relative in London, came to see her practically every day after work to cheer her up and remained with her until she was ready to go to bed so that no-one else had to be called.

To show some appreciation on her aunt's behalf, she ordered flowers to be delivered to the house. That evening, she was just approaching the front door, when Agnes intercepted her.

"Miss Dorothy, there was no need to do this, but thank you very much all the same. Look how artistically Bella has arranged them in one of the Chinese vases."

Relaxed, with a winning smile on her face now that the day's work was behind her, she switched the light on in the deserted dining-room.

"You look so pale, young lady. Bella and I were talking about you only a few minutes ago. Nothing bad, of course! We were saying that none of our guests' children are as concerned about their parent's welfare as you are about your aunt's. Please forgive me, if you feel I am being nosy. Have you had a proper meal today?" And, scrutinizing the slim, small person, she answered her own question, "no, not today and probably not many other days. Allow me to heat something up. It won't take a minute. Come."

The sincerity of Agnes's words and sudden pangs of hunger prompted the young woman to follow Agnes into the kitchen. There, breakfast trays covered with spotless white cloths, the necessary cutlery, plates, cups, jugs and jam-pots were aligned on two-tier trolleys.

Bella, now more modestly attired, was bending over blue silk material, spread out on the large kitchen table, tracing round the edges of a pattern; piles of bills were stacked in one corner.

"My untidy book-keeping," admitted Agnes. "Our long-suffering accountant took pity on us when we first started the business. I would be in a right muddle without him."

With the back of one hand she swept the papers into an empty saucepan which she held at the edge of the table with the other hand.

"Now there is enough space for your plate."

Within ten minutes she produced a warm meal.

"This is my favourite hour: my staff has gone; the guests are upstairs."

With a sigh of relief, she proceeded to a well-worn armchair by the window. The old Singer sewing machine stood next to it. She switched on the light, slumped into the chair and kicked an old pouffe under her swollen legs.

"Ach, das tut gut! (This really feels good)."

The day's strains and stresses were forgotten; unfinished menus, staff rota, shopping lists and so much more were shelved until the morning. With her bulky body in repose and her white, glossy hair shimmering in the lamp's ray of light, her features radiated tenderness.

Mrs Goldmann had shed her landlady's mantle until daybreak; she had reverted to Agnes, her private self. Dorothy stared incredulously at the other Mrs Goldmann, who could have easily been anyone's grandmother.

"It wasn't always that hard, Miss Dorothy," Agnes said gently. "In business you have to be tough, sometimes even unpleasant, in order to survive."

Bella, taciturn and seemingly absorbed in cutting round the paper pattern, made as much noise as she could. She rattled the pin box, pushed the dummy back and forth, stamped her feet and tutted with impatience. She did so again and again when Dorothy whiled away a couple of hours with the sisters after visiting her aunt.

Gradually the young girl realized that Bella resented her intrusion; passive resistance was the weapon she had chosen with which to punish Agnes for letting an outsider into their, at least outwardly, self-sufficient existence. Bella was obsessed with her sister, craving for her sole attention. She was totally unsure of herself in spite of her superb performance as a consummate hostess when in contact with the guests and their relatives.

That is why Dorothy tried, but never succeeded, in stealing unnoticed past the kitchen door. Agnes would lie in wait for her; as if the young woman's company filled a gap in her otherwise busy life.

Bella, in a huff, would stalk out after ten minutes,

snapping in a high-pitched voice, "I'm going to bed now. Don't switch on the light in our bedroom. I will be fast asleep."

Agnes would invariably repeat in a resigned tone, "Please forgive her rude manners. She is extremely insecure, even jealous. I have never been able to make real friends. She cold-shoulders anyone in whom I take the slightest interest. She was even jealous of my son; she is like a clinging vine."

"It is a burden to be the eldest child," Agnes said the following day. "Twelve years is a very big gap and all her life Bella has treated me as her guide and mentor, not so our dear, unsophisticated mother, who gave into her every whim, while our father paid a fortune for riding, singing and dancing lessons. I must admit that she was a beautiful child...She still hasn't lost her good looks, has she, Dorothy?"

The young woman was just about to answer when Agnes added, "since her late teens it was always "Agnes, what do you think?" "What shall I wear?" "What shall I do?" Her need of my approval and advice cost me the love of my son who is only a few years her junior. After my husband died in 1929...oh, so long ago," she sighed. "After my husband died the bond between Bella and me grew ever stronger. Martin felt I was neglecting him and punished me by accepting a research fellowship in America. A couple of years later, I was informed by friends that he had married. No invitation was sent to me."

Over many weeks fragments of their inseparable lives were calmly narrated. Before referring to her own feelings, Agnes always carefully weighed every word in an effort to be objective. At no time did Dorothy detect a trace of bitterness.

She did not dare to voice what was puzzling her. Why had she, a complete stranger, been chosen to become the custodian of this intimate family history?

One day, when least expected, Agnes provided the answer. "I am treating you as the sensitive, feeling grandchild I have always wished for. Please don't blush, Dorothy. I have never before told my secret thoughts so freely" and, looking straight into her eyes, "let them be in your safe-keeping, and yours alone."

Words failed her; none in Dorothy's vocabulary was really adequate enough to express her empathy and guarantee her discretion.

"Nothing has really changed between us," Agnes went on. "Bella still comes first. She is almost part of me. All I ever did or said was in her best interests."

Seamlessly, she moved to the next part: Bella's unsuccessful marriage in 1920 to Liebermann. "The young man arrived on the scene from America, the land of untold riches, so he made her believe, an aphrodisiac to my sister. He gambled, lost, recouped his losses, overwhelming her with expensive gifts and fantastic tales about his family's wealth. Had she not been groomed for such a suitor? Her dream had come true. But under that smooth veneer lurked a vain, arrogant, insufferable confidence trickster who was only intent on winning the hand of the prosperous merchant's daughter. I warned her; she hated me for it. During that phase of her life she had no need of me.

"Better keep an eye on your financially incompetent husband," she jeered, "if you cannot enjoy with me the happiest days of my life."

I had to stand by, powerless, as my young sister sacrificed

her innocence to this brute of a man. They married; divorce papers were filed one year later. The wedding night, she confessed, had been a horrific nightmare. The groom's perverse behaviour had petrified his bride."

She moved her elbows on the side-supports of the armchair, placed her chin in cupped hands and closed her eyes for a moment. Then she whispered, "I don't want to upset you with my poor sister's graphic descriptions."

When she had regained her composure, she continued, having realized that the inexperienced young woman lapped up Bella's story because she felt it was as intriguing as any of the novels she had read.

"Within a week she was back with Mother. He had frittered away his own funds and had lost Bella's dowry playing poker. For a brief period he even had the audacity to expect my parents to keep them both in style. But the inflation in the early twenties of the 20th century had made a beggar of my father. He could have papered the walls of their flat with worthless bank notes. A heart attack took him from us; Mother only survived him a few months. As paternal financial sources had dried up, her husband did not trouble Bella any more; they were divorced.

"However, my sister bore a permanent scar. She had lost complete faith in her own judgment; she was unable to cope on her own. Finally I asked her to come and live with us; the furniture of my parents' home was sold, except for a few pieces which had stood in Bella's bedroom."

Week after week more episodes followed one another in almost chronological order. It seemed that Agnes prepared them mentally like a script-writer, leaving open-endings quite unintentionally. That had made Dorothy a keener listener.

Did it ever occur to Bella that her sister would be capable of recreating their past, giving away something so intimate to the young woman whom she considered a trespasser into their very private domain? And what would happen if she decided to pad silently down the stairs and catch her sister out? These were questions Dorothy turned over and over in her mind until she concluded that she, if nothing else, was party to some form of auto-therapy, as Agnes reviewed and explained to herself the stranglehold which tied her to her sibling.

"What was I to do with my sister?"

She threw out this rhetorical question, as if an appropriate solution had eluded her.

"After that dreadful divorce there was nothing she could do, except sing really well. To lift her out of her moral morass she took up singing lessons again to retrain her voice. *Chansons* were her forte; thanks to her teacher's connections she was offered engagements to appear in cabaret.

There was no one less suited to be an *artiste* than Bella. She would only perform if I was sitting within eye-contact near the stage, metaphorically holding her hands to steady her nerves. As soon as her act was over she would come to my table, ungraciously rejecting any admirers who sought closer acquaintance.

"At first this was considered to be a capricious ruse; but her career came to an abrupt end when it became evident that the ravishing lady refused to entertain the *clientèle* after hours. Her behaviour on stage belied her modesty."

A broad smile spread over Agnes's deeply furrowed face, as she enlightened Dorothy about the atmosphere in Berlin's night-life during the Twenties.

"Morals were so low in artistic circles; cabaret *artistes*

were deemed to be fair game, not only by male but also female predators."

She interrupted her flow to ascertain whether the young woman caught the drift. And, further warming to her subject, she said, "even a famous actress, Adele S., over twice Bella's age, propositioned my sister and pursued her. I will never forget her employer's parting shot. "Little lady, we have not engaged you for your act alone, however delightful this may be. If you cannot defrost yourself and comply with our patrons' expectations I am very sorry, my dear *chanteuse*, that I have to terminate your engagement as from tonight. You leave me no alternative."

Dorothy, who had been raised in a puritan atmosphere before studying in a Church of England college, listened spellbound to the unravelling of the sisters' colourful trajectory through what used to be called The Roaring Twenties. Stimulated by her appreciative audience, Agnes painted a vivid canvas, adding shadows and high- lights in order to heighten the effect. And everything centred round Bella, as if her young sibling were her alter ego, the focal point of her life.

It was fortunate that Miss Talbot was preoccupied with her own problems. For the straight-laced spinster would have been appalled had she got wind of these nightly confessionals. Family secrets, she had insisted, should be kept behind closed doors; eavesdropping was despicable in her eyes.

As the weeks slipped by, Agnes's auto- biographical narrative finally reached the early Thirties. With profound emotion she described the rise of Hitler, the impact it had on German Jews and how they were ostracized. Having lost her husband so recently, as well as being responsible for her 'baby' sister, it was a traumatic period.

"That reminds me of one particular afternoon when I had taken my little sister to the zoo. She was fascinated by the deer. "Oh, all these Bambis with their light brown fur and white spots on their back. Look at this one; he is completely white! The poor animal is not with the others; they have turned their backs towards him; he must feel very sad."

During our walk home she would not stop talking about the albino deer who grazed all by himself in the enclosure. And it made me wonder whether even in the animal world a creature is rejected by the herd merely because its colour and markings are different from the others."

"During that same period the other flat on our landing changed hands," said Agnes, embarking on another chapter of Bella's ill-fated love-life.

"Peter Schulz and his mother, the new tenants, blue-eyed, tall, blond - her hair may have been retouched - were perfect epitomes of the 'Aryan' race, according to Hitler's new racial theories. They were refined, courteous people and respectful to us, in spite of our marked Jewish features. (According to the racial laws, Jews belonged to a subhuman species.) Soon it became only too obvious that the young man devised discreet schemes to establish daily contact with my sister. He seemed to watch her from their window; when she went out, I heard him chasing downstairs in order to overtake her.

"One Friday morning a bouquet of red roses was delivered. The attached little card inside bore Bella's name. This was the first time for a few years that she had received flowers. Her excitement was catching, though I had forebodings.

"Would you consider it too forward, if I were to ask you to do me the honour of accompanying me to the opera tomorrow night?" He wrote with a firm hand; the wording of the message was a reflection of his respectability and high principles.

"Together we composed an acceptance note which she dropped into his letter box. The effect it had on her was breathtaking. In spite of her age, she behaved like a young debutante before her coming-out dance. For several hours she tried on and discarded dresses, shoes and accessories from her over-flowing wardrobe, before she settled on the most flattering evening gown.

"Does it still suit me, Agnes?" "Is this lipstick too red or is there too much rouge on my cheeks?"

"It was as if the clock had been turned back many years. I was happy that his attraction to her was beginning to restore some of her self-confidence; yet I had great misgivings about this budding relationship.

Jews were more and more marginalized. Christians who mixed with us socially were frowned upon. And to make matters worse, Peter held a position as a legal adviser in local government.

"He was stunned when he called for her that evening. His handsome, features glowed with pleasure. Their friendship deepened and his genuine love for her broke down the invisible wall Bella had built round herself.

"Disaster struck much sooner than I had anticipated. He did not fall out of love but he, too, had to abide by the law which prohibited association between Jews and Gentiles. I remember only too well that Sunday afternoon when he rang the bell to break the painful news with great sadness in his demeanour and voice.

"Bella, dearest, I am heartbroken," he said in front of me, "but I have to swim with the tide for my mother's sake. This is just for now, darling; I will always love you. We both have to wait patiently, for this government will not last. History has taught us that all dictators come to a bitter end. When this ill-wind has blown over, you with your sister and all our Jewish compatriots will be welcomed back into their homeland."

"Warning that worse was to come in the near future, he begged us to leave before more stringent emigration laws came into force. Peter took Bella, whose body was shaking, into his arms for the last time; then he left us, bewildered and shattered. My sister collapsed. The man she had learned to love had deserted her. How was it that my lovely little sister always lost out?"

She fell silent. With her right elbow on the arm-rest, she cushioned her tilted head in the palm of her hand, closed her eyes and looked inwards.

Then an afterthought stirred her.

"Peter did us a great service. Exposing himself to the utmost danger, his warning motivated us not to delay our departure any longer."

Eventually Miss Talbot's leg had mended sufficiently for her to walk by herself with the aid of a stick. A few weeks later she was able to resume again her manifold interests away from the home.

This coincided with the first signs of Bella's terminal illness. No consultant in the length and breadth of Harley Street diagnosed what was really wrong with her. Instead, they came to the conclusion among themselves that they were dealing with a neurotic, self-centered woman in her early forties who refused to accept her age. What specialists failed to establish, a young doctor, a locum, identified after his first examination. An ambulance took her to the nearest hospital.

Every visiting hour Agnes could be found at her sister's bedside in hospital. A few weeks passed; the sick woman was discharged as incurable. Her sister could not sleep at night in the room they shared. She watched her constantly, tormented by the grief, she succeeded in hiding, as her sister wasted away.

Dorothy became aware of the gloom which pervaded the whole house. The well-trained staff had taken over. All the guests moved about quietly, frightened of what would become of them.

Bella passed away a few months later. On the day of the funeral Agnes and her son escorted the hearse to the top of the road: a ritual performed by chief mourners, according to Jewish tradition. The burial was attended by Dorothy together with all the guests and the staff. Everyone returned home afterwards; there was no reception.

Agnes, distraught, sat in her armchair by the kitchen window.

"My son is already in consultation with my solicitor and accountant. He is like a stranger to me and of no comfort. How could I know," she lamented, "that Bella's stomach had become so swollen because of advanced cancer? In my ignorance and, hoping to cheer her up, I used to say, "It's like being pregnant without a lover"."

With her eyes conveying grief and desolation, she spoke of her sister's last five months, a catalogue of sheer torture;

in vain, everything was tried to preserve her a little longer.
"I could not contemplate life without her," she repeated over and over again.

The day after the funeral Martin, a man of action in the American mould, requested that everyone in the house should assemble in the lounge at five o'clock. The room had been rearranged to seat residents in upholstered chairs in the front rows; Mary, Tony, Cook and her helpers on kitchen chairs at the back.

The son, as if he were about to address his company's lower orders, surveyed the   gathering facing him: the old people still in shock, his grief-stricken mother and the all the staff, apprehensive about their job security.

"In view of my aunt's death," he began coldly, as if he were addressing his firm's lower orders, "I have decided to put this property on the market. My mother's poor mental and physical condition leave me with no other alternative."

His dispassionate address hit the old people like a thunderbolt. They stared at him, devastated by what they had heard.

"Mother told me that without her sister, her life-long companion, she has no will to carry on. She is now relying on me to sort out her affairs. I regret to have to spring this new development on you today. Guests and staff will be given three months' notice. It should give you enough time to make other arrangements."

He paused, scanning their faces to make sure that his words had been clearly understood, especially by the bewildered old people who had hoped to spend the rest of their days in the same environment.

"You cannot but agree that this is a generous gesture on my part. I thought you would prefer to know what is in store for you before estate agents attach the 'FOR SALE' board to the garden gate."

Agnes, shrunk in stature, sat immobile and voiceless in her chair. Tears tricked down her ashen face.

"It's pointless appealing to my mother. She is a spent force. I have booked a room for her in one of the most reputable registered Jewish nursing homes which might meet your needs," he concluded in an officious manner.

No muscle moved in his mother's face. Her body and soul clad in mourning, she was oblivious of the here and now. The residents, forgetting their own plight just for an instant, wondered whether their formerly indomitable hostess realized that her fate had been sealed.

* * *

Now a mature woman, able to assess the influences and turning-points in her own life, Dorothy was gripped by a nagging desire to gain admittance to what was once Agnes's domain.

The estate agent fixed an appointment with the present owners on the following Sunday to let her view the property. She went up the crumbling steps leading to the front door and stood rigid as she inspected the windowsills, white-washed in former years. They were covered with mould and thick layers of pigeon droppings. The flowerbed along the broken path was overgrown with weeds; the façade of the house needed pointing; paint had flaked off the pipes and rust had set in.

An old man answered the bell. She stated her business. He asked her to come in. Unconcerned, he lumbered back into the kitchen, leaving Dorothy in the hall. The stained glass panels of the inner doors were in place; encrusted grime concealed the designs. All around her was dank and grey, the old carpet threadbare.

"You're free to walk around. Sorry, it's all in a bit of a mess."

The voice belonged to a young woman in long drapes and tangled hair. "Nothing much has been done to this house for ye-e-e-ars." She drew out the vowels to underline the length of time.

The lounge was cluttered with shabby furniture; the parquet floor, overlaid with frayed mats, was almost black; spiders crawling out of the many plaster cracks in the grey ceiling had spun their webs un- disturbed.

"What is missing is Miss Haversham," crossed Dorothy's mind.

Saddened by what she saw and a lump in her throat, she proceeded along the hall into the kitchen, which had always been immaculately clean.

"One must be able to eat off the floor," had been the house motto.

Greasy splotches spattered the grimy wall at the back of the cooker; the white six-burner (over which Agnes had slaved away with sweat on her brow) was now discoloured by dried, yellowish specks of grease. Brown watermarks trailed down from the ceiling; mildew grew round the rotting window-frames near where Agnes used to sit after the day's work was done.

"There's a garden at the back. Go through the utility room on the left," the young woman called out from the hall.

This had been Agnes's larder; it was filled with junk over which Dorothy stepped cautiously in order to get outside. Who had uprooted the rose bushes? What had happened to the lawn, the ornamental stone vases and the carefully tended flowerbeds? It was a wilderness, except for the coarse grass, festooned with dark pants and bras which had fallen off the washing-line.

Dorothy retreated into the kitchen.

"Thank you, I have seen enough."

Neither the old man, reading at the kitchen table, nor the girl at the filthy sink favoured her with a look.

She exited through the neglected front door and hurried along the weed-choked path. Not once did she look back; lest she were to blot out the vision of the impressive property with its quaint elegant *décor* of two decades ago, or should erase the memories she had shared with Agnes, Bella's faithful guardian, the indomitable mistress of the house.

The Poetess

"He didn't want my baby," she wailed, when she sat down. "He didn't want MY baby, *der Schuft* (the bastard)," she exclaimed forcefully. The other diners in the restaurant turned their heads towards our table.

Ulrike, emotionally charged, reverted to her native tongue as she was talking to me about her ex-husband, although she had made it a priority to perfect her English during her twenty years residence in this country. However, she cultivated a slight German accent, "so that people would remember me better," as she put it.

There had been, and still was, no need for this. Among the three hundred odd parents who had sent their children to the school for physically handicapped pupils where I taught, she would have stood out. Her straight, shoulder-length hair was corn-blond, her eyes deep blue. Her features were singularly mobile: pathetic, imperious or regal; her rouged lips, either soft or obstinately pressed together, as the occasion demanded. She wore elegant, expensive garments with an almost *risqué décolletage*.

At our very first encounter she looked too young to be the mother of, Hermann, her eight-year-old son who had the body of a teenager. Ill-wishers among the staff bred rumours that the boy was at least three to four years older. According to them, she had falsified the date of his birth for some wanton reason. She politely explained to the head that the original certificate had been lost abroad. Always a consummate fantasist, she reshaped the truth to suit her purpose.

The school doctor, who had examined the boy after

enrolment, also thought Hermann Kütner was eleven years old, not three years younger, as his mother would have us believe. The child was slim, much taller than the others in his class: head and shoulders above them with long legs, sitting erect in his electric wheelchair. Like his mother, he had corn-coloured hair; the fringe, hiding his high brow, almost touched his blue eyes. They stared out of his pale face at the strange surroundings into which he had been planted at his mother's behest.

"Come and have a chat with my new pupil," my colleague said to me a couple of days after his arrival. "I cannot get a word out of him. No one had warned me that he cannot speak English and my school German does not elicit any response."

Hermann withdrew deeper into the chair, a reddish hue flushing over his face when I addressed him. I was invading his privacy. Yet, when I spoke to him about the town in which I had been raised before WWII and where his mother lived, he leaned forward and listened to me intently without uttering a single word.

As the weeks went by he, a very intelligent lad, started to communicate with the adults, due to tuition paid for by his mother. He did not mix with his peers or any older pupil; during play-time, he observed them from a distance, his eyes following the trajectory of a ball or studying the way they managed to handle a hockey stick. After a while even the most kind-hearted of them who had encouraged him to partake in their games, left him alone.

Frau Ulrike Kütner, a renowned poetess, spent more time in Germany than in her Kensington apartment in London. During her absence, her widowed mother was in charge of him. She spoke to me frequently while waiting in the entrance hall to drive her grandson to a psychiatrist. (This had been recommended by the school's social worker.)

"He feels displaced; not that he was very happy in the boarding-school in Germany. Most weekends he spent with us. I treat him most affectionately, but he does not reciprocate my love. As for my daughter, something must have snapped in her mental make-up when she saw the deformed baby. I cannot detect a natural bond between mother and child."

On each occasion she apologized profusely for delaying me, always adding, "There is no one in whom I can confide. My neighbours are strangers; friends at home are busy with their own problems. My daughter pretends her son is happy and that our little family is living in harmony.

"Ulrike is an absentee mother. Even when she is with us, her feet are never on the ground. My taciturn grandson never reveals what is on his mind. When his father visits us, the unpleasant atmosphere is unbearable. The child overhears his parents' quarrels. They blame each other for the failure of their marriage."

Such a quarrel blew up in school under the embarrassing circumstances. Both parents had been summoned to attend a meeting by the headmistress in the presence of the school doctor. What had been discussed behind closed doors must have agitated them intensively. Yet, they decided to join their son for lunch in the hall, sitting on either side of him.

Kitchen staff served the meals. The usual chatter of the boys and girls was abruptly silenced. Hermann's parents had started a heated argument in German, a language the pupils did not understand. They turned their heads towards the couple, while the son, literally caught up in the middle, kept quiet; tears trickled down his face. Then, seeing his distress, the pair left after apologizing profusely to the head and the staff who had witnessed the unpleasant scene.

The following morning at break, I saw his grandmother closing the Head's door.

"I said to her," she told me, "that I was sorry for the unacceptable way his parents behaved in the school hall and the effect it had on that poor lad. Neither of them can handle the dilemma which has faced them since the birth of the child.

"My daughter was born after my fortieth birthday. My late husband and I reproached ourselves for the fundamental mistakes we made when we raised her. My generation grew up under such different circumstances in the thirties and the war years. Our views on child-rearing were completely out of date; we were too set in our ways to move on.

"Ulrike was a dreamer in her early years, quite happy on her own, always composing verses. Oh, we were so proud when she dedicated them to us on birthdays and anniversaries. After her seventeenth birthday, my husband and I were approaching our sixtieth birthdays. We felt we should find her a husband among our younger acquaintances. We did not want her to be on her own when we had passed away. I was reasonably fit, but her father had never been strong: the war years had taken their toll.

"Erich, Hermann's father in his early thirties, was a junior consultant in my husband's clinic. Over the years they had become close friends. He had known our daughter since childhood, and we realized that he was struck by her beauty, watching her whenever he was with us at home and at parties. He was a committed bachelor but fell head over heels in love with her. It did not surprise us at all when he asked us for her hand. We were delighted. It was a great weight off our shoulders."

The sound of the school bell drew me back to the classroom. She held on to me, and sighing deeply, she said, "Please just let me finish. Ulrike was not ready to be a wife. We talked her into it. What's done cannot be undone. That poor child is paying a high price for it."

After these last words she let me go.

Hermann's grandmother must have returned to Germany because I did not see her any more after that day. The boy left our school because his mother had found a boarding-school for handicapped senior pupils, which allowed her to return to Germany whenever necessary.

* * *

Several years passed. Somehow Ulrike learned about my retirement party on the last day of the summer term. She breezed in just as I was packing up, dressed in a light blue silk garment, took the presents I had been given by pupils' parents and offered to drive me home.

"May I visit you before I fly back? My mother thought so highly of you and advised me to keep in touch with you. Sadly, she has passed away. I sincerely regret I was too absorbed in my career to realize that she, in her high seventies, should have enjoyed the evening of her life; instead, she was burdened by such a great responsibility. It never occurred to me I would miss her so much. I should have tried harder to be with them, to get closer to my son and show my mother how much I loved her. It is too late now."

Her grave look confirmed that her words were genuine.

A month later she came to my house.

"May I tell you what happened when I first got married?"

Immediately I recalled the intimate remarks her mother had made.

"Mine was a union of an immature teenager with a man almost twice my age, a man with a dual personality: the serious professional my parents related to and the man-about-town with many affairs behind him; they had no knowledge about an illegitimate child somewhere in the north.

With hindsight, I was a sacrificial lamb given to him as a gesture of friendship."

I was prepared for a long session and had put a plate of assorted pastries on the table in front of the sofa. After brewing the tea, I sat beside her. Every so often, trying to recall the sequence of events, Ulrike had a sip and ate some cake.

"In the sleeping compartment in the train which took us on our honeymoon across Southern Germany to the French Alps, my young, uninitiated self had the first rude awakening. Erich, well-versed in what he called 'the art of love' with experienced partners, had no idea how to be gentle with an innocent like me. And all at such close quarters; I could not escape his big paws undressing me unceremoniously, throwing my elegant lace wedding-dress down, as if it were a rag. Without the slightest inkling of my anxiety he touched me, though my whole body trembled. He asserted his marital rights. I passed out."

She shuddered and pushed the open palms of her hands

forward to ward off an invisible rapist, her face distorted with fear.

It was impossible to know whether she had embroidered the facts or whether her strange behaviour was merely intended to lend credence to the 'rape scene' she had so vividly described. With her keen perception, she guessed that I harboured doubts about the honest truth of every bit of her recollections.

"My memory of the brutality with which he handled me during the wedding-night has not been clouded by the passage of time."

"How did he react?"

"He is a doctor. It did not take long to bring me round. Then, I covered my face to hide my tears and stifle any noise.

In the morning I managed to compose myself. It seemed like a nightmare, not reality, once we had breakfast in the dining-car. To the outside world, we appeared to be a charming couple.

"At Annecy we transferred to a local train to take us to our destination, La Clusaz. He pretended to be the solicitous husband of a young wife, completely different from the man who, and I am not exaggerating, had raped me during the night."

La Clusaz, where I had spent memorable holidays with my family, nestles at the foot of the Aravis mountain range; high rocks zigzag above what was then a quiet little resort, favoured by French holiday makers. It was exceptional to hear any foreign language spoken.

In late autumn the forest, leading to the town, is at its most beautiful when the sun shines through the brown, golden, russet and yellow leaves. The couple arrived there during that same season, and it was in this poetic setting that the tragedy unfolded in the summer of the following year.

"The scenery was so wonderful. We walked arm-in-arm along the paths like any happy newly-weds as soon as we had unpacked. I willed myself to enjoy the moment. The dreaded night was still many hours away.

When we returned, the garden behind the hotel was alive with other guests. They were enjoying the still mild weather after the accustomed after-lunch rest upstairs. In the centre, middle-aged men and women played *boules*, a French version of bowls. My husband was fascinated; he stood at the edge of the long oblong pitch, dying to join the game.

He cheered when a *boule* had managed to dislodge those of the opposite team and had landed nearest to the small, white ball; I forget the correct name. Erich cheered until his enthusiasm was noticed by the players. One of them brought down a spare set and explained the rudimentary rules in simple terms which he understood.

"Every afternoon the men acted like schoolboys playing their favourite game; if a team were short of players, a wife with a modicum of skill would be press-ganged to make up the numbers. I chatted with the ladies, all of them older than I, practicing what *mademoiselle* had taught me in school. They passed on the pitfalls of married life and how to avoid them. The matrons were full of admiration for my 'charming, educated' husband. Little did they know him and how I dreaded the onset of dusk. It heralded a repetition of another 'invasion of my body' similar to what I had endured. We left after a fortnight, having promised we would return the next year with Erich's own set of *boules*."

* * *

She looked at her watch; she had been talking for nearly an hour.

"You are all right for time, or shall I come back another day?"

I assured her that she could carry on. She was rather longwinded in what followed with many digressions, as was her wont.

"We went home to Erich's bachelor apartment, refurbished and renovated during our absence according to his and my parents' taste. My husband informed me that he would not change his lifestyle: playing tennis, bridge evenings with his friends, including my parents, when he was not on call at the clinic during his weekends off.

"Of course you are very welcome, dear," he repeated at frequent intervals. "You can watch us and learn the rules. As soon as you have mastered them you can partake."

"We went to parties, usually reunions of colleagues. Although I was treated as an adult, the women present overwhelmed me with the dangers of childbirth. They advised me on the choice of nannies."

She complained about being left daily in the company of his servants who had taken any housewifely duties off her shoulders, as befitted a lady of her class and his status. She felt lonely; again she took refuge in what gave her the greatest satisfaction: giving free rein to her imagination in verses. These she kept out of sight in a locked drawer of her dressing-table for fear of being ridiculed by her husband. Finally, in a bold move for someone so timid and unworldly, she searched for and found a publisher who was willing to take on her collection of poems in a small, limited edition with artwork on the cover, provided she shared the cost of publicity and distribution.

Not one member of her family had been privy to her daring venture. The first time they heard of it was when they read reviews in literary supplements, praising the work of a newly discovered young poetess. The success at last enhanced her standing in the family's circle of friends. Even her husband was impressed by the wife whose inner life he hardly knew or had made any effort to get to know, or had taken seriously.

Ulrike became pregnant; the anticipated birth was at the beginning of September. Erich had booked their holiday in the same resort and hotel for the second and third weeks of August; they would meet again their French friends. After having been cloistered in the clinic for almost ten months, he was eager to breathe the Alpine air, keen to try out his new *boules* with the other *affectionados* of the game.

"I am going to be very uncomfortable in the heat, carrying the extra weight. Could we not spend the two weeks nearer home in one of the beauty spots along the Rhine, instead of being abroad in a small town at the top of a mountain?" she pointed out.

"Have you forgotten that I am a doctor, speaking fluent French? So what are you worried about?" he retorted angrily.

She did not mention to him that he had never, during his whole career, delivered a baby, for fear of causing another dreadful confrontation. They usually ended up in tears and underlined his unwillingness to make any concessions, even though this was one of the rare instances when Ulrike was supported by her mother. Her father, as usual, sided with her husband. It threw a shadow over her parents' long and loving marriage.

On their arrival in La Clusaz, they were greeted by the hotel's guests, all of them middle-aged, except for an invalid daughter in her thirties. She had come again with her parents. Ulrike had little in common with her. Everyone was appalled that the expectant mother's health and that of the unborn baby had been exposed to such a risk. They kept it to themselves.

Erich enjoyed himself as he had done the previous year, *insouciant* of Ulrike's increasing discomfort until the second Sunday evening. Her pain had become unbearable: the unborn had shifted. On examining her, he knew that the birth was imminent.

This was one of the most important days in the year, *Le Jour de Fête*. Inhabitants and holiday-makers alike were out and about. On improvised stages, brass bands played familiar tunes.

The only doctor in the small resort was away; the locum could not be found. *Monsieur* Dubois, the *hotelier*, took pity on the distressed couple. With Eric by his side, he drove down the mountain to two lower small resorts in the hope that the only other doctor practicing in the area was available. He, too, was not at home. When they returned Ulrike, white-faced with red rings round her tear-sodden eyes, was lying on the bed trying to shield the swollen abdomen with her hands. The contractions had become ever more frequent and severe.

Time being at a premium, Erich made a snap decision. He carried his wife, her hands clasped round his neck and her legs supported by his hip-bones and, as gently as possible, he manoeuvred her into the car and jumped in beside her. *Monsieur* Dubois drove off to Annecy, the largest town, dodging laughing crowds in festive mood. All this happened before mobile phones had been invented. The telephone exchange had been inundated with callers; there had been no opportunity to alert the hospital of the urgent need to admit a woman in labour.

The *hotelier*, dodging round anyone in his way, dashed to the reception desk. His manner and words were enough to convince the matron, who happened to be passing by, that the mother-to-be needed immediate attention.

Ulrike's waters broke while she was lifted carefully on to the hospital trolley. She lost consciousness as they wheeled her into the theatre. The obstetrician and his team were waiting for her.

Her husband and *Monsieur* Dubois had been shown into the waiting-room; they sat in silence. It was the very first time in his adult life that Erich, the well-respected clinician, was not in control. He would never be again in his marriage.

An hour slipped by. Erich peered through the door's window. Nurses with medical passed along the corridor. Eventually the obstetrician-in-charge appeared.

"Who is the father?"

"I am," Ulrike's husband said quietly;
He stood up like a schoolboy, ready to be
chastised by the master.

"We managed to save your baby son. Your wife lost a lot of blood and is under sedation. It is my sad duty to inform you that the baby is paralysed from the waist down due to a difficult delivery. I wonder if your wife has been examined regularly, especially during the last month."

The obstetrician's tone was grave and reproachful.

"I understand that you are on holiday high up in the

mountains with no nursing facilities. Under the circumstances your wife and baby will be with us for at least another two weeks under observation. At the moment it seems doubtful that she will be fit enough to travel once she has been discharged. You may visit your wife and your son tomorrow."

It hit Erich like a bomb-shell. Every one of his plans had been ruined, including the celebration in a five-star hotel. Besides, his deputy expected him back at work. In sheer desperation, he rang his parents-in-law in the morning to inform them of the sad news. Ulrike's mother took the first available plane; she was at her bedside by late-afternoon the following day.

Ulrike repeated to me what she had heard from her mother. Before, during and after the birth, she had been too ill to really know what was happening to her.

"What a relief it was to see my mother! It did not matter to me that Erich had gone home. Owing to her presence, I became stronger. Both of us were devastated by my baby's incurable condition. After all, I was still so young. How was I to cope with the tragedy facing me for the rest of my life? All my hopes, and those of my parents, were shattered.

"You had a baby yourself, so you can appreciate what I felt when all the other mothers showed off their new-born with perfectly formed limbs. And the more I began to understand the extent of the handicap, as well as what the future had in store for him and for me, the greater grew my resentment: I began to hate Eric; I still believe he was to blame. Due to his sheer negligence my son has to suffer for the whole of his life; I, at his side, have to watch helplessly.

"They discharged me after two more weeks. Every day my husband had been ringing. I refused to speak to him and begged my mother to do likewise. But she is of the old school; she reminded me over and over again that Erich must play a part in his life."

During the return flight, aware that her marriage had been a disaster for all concerned (she did not even want to face her husband any more), Ulrike decided that henceforth she would live again in her parental home; a live-in nurse would care for her son. She would sue for divorce on account of cruelty or his extra marital affairs. Of the latter she had no valid proof.

"In vain my parents tried to talk me out of it. They begged me to speak with him when he called with a bunch of red roses on our arrival. I refused. I had made up my mind to stay with my parents until I was old enough to fend for my son and myself."

Trying to justify herself, she spared no details about the unprofessional live-in nurses who took charge of the baby. The first one was more concerned about her comforts than those of the baby; the second had a short temper, was noisy and did not get on with the family; the third had a drink problem.

Her elderly parents could not put up with the disruption to their former tranquil existence. It took its toll on her father, in particular. He tried to act, unsuccessfully, as a go-between for the young wife and her husband. Finally it was agreed that Hermann should be cared for in a home for handicapped children.

Ulrike confessed that she was relieved to be spared daily contact with her son. It was her mother who hardly missed a day from seeing her grandson. In time she, in the growing child's perception, became the only person he would trust.

Ulrike's father took a mere bit-player part in the baby's life.

Once again Ulrike spent most of her waking hours locked in the room, her sanctuary ever since childhood. Much of what she had experienced was mirrored in her poems. By the time she became of age (at twenty-one in those days), her work had found some acclaim; her second collection won prodigious prizes. She became well-known, not only for her books, but for the tragic story of her young life. In women's magazines, photos on the covers presented her as a beautiful, tragic heroine. An expert in exploiting all the publicity on offer, though stopping short of causing her husband any undue embarrassment or anything which might harm his brilliant career, she wallowed in it.

Being financially independent, she had rented an apartment in a fashionable area of the town, furnished to her own taste and away from her parents' vigilant and enquiring eyes. Her mother and father had tried to provide a safety-net for her which, she complained, throttled her.

As Hermann grew older, his mother felt emotionally strong enough to get closer to him; however nerve-wracking it proved to be at first. She noticed that the boy began to feel some affection for her. Hesitantly, he started to respond to questions; he had inherited his father's intelligence and his mother's interest in literature. He was able to read at an early age. Being a loner in any group, he spent his free time in books. That inspired Ulrike to write children's poems dedicated to him. Her precious gift to him was the key which unlocked a slowly growing relationship; it flourished in years to come: mainly on an intellectual level. Their past experiences had eroded their capacity to love: both fearing future rejection.

"What decided you to bring your son to us in London? How old was he then?"

Ulrike did not reply straight away, ignoring my second question completely. She was not quite sure how many years she had subtracted from his age when she had initially enrolled him.

"I have turned into an out-and-out free spirit; in Germany educational authorities are behind the times. The *régime* in the boarding-school was far too strict for my liking: too little regard for the individual's needs or talents. The English school was highly recommended by an acquaintance, an eminent paediatrician. So I travelled to London and went to an estate agent near Harrods; I had heard that it was a superior store. Without my parents' and Erich knowledge, I bought the three-bedroom flat, had it redecorated, furnished it and brought my mother over for her approval.

"No doubt Erich had a right to be consulted beforehand. But as far as I was concerned, his opinion did not carry any weight with me. Luckily, having been promoted to replace my father, he had even less time for the welfare of his son.

"Hermann, away from the constraints of the German school, felt liberated. What to me is so important: he takes a great interest in my career. Miraculously, he, too, pours all his suppressed emotions into the most imaginative poetic stories."

At last Ulrike was anchored; so was her son. Her mother, now a widow, stayed in London when she publicized her books or discussed matters with her publisher. But when she felt unable to shoulder the responsibility of looking after her mid- teenage grandson any longer she returned to Germany.

Christine Smith, the maid, trustworthy and gentle and only four years older than her son, was perfectly capable to cope with his handicap. She had cared for her wheelchair-bound grandmother who had always lived with the family.
She moved into the spare bedroom and efficiently managed, with little direction, all the household chores. Within a short time she became fond of the boy. Together they went to the Kensington stores or Hyde Park. Ulrike could not believe her luck in having engaged such a committed help.

For many months contact between us stopped altogether. I was surprised when I heard her voice again on the telephone.
"Even now I miss my mother, so does Hermann. He has achieved the required marks and has been offered a place at university.
By the way, Christine still lives with me, as a friend. She is a teacher's assistant in a special school after a one-year course which she passed with flying colours. In her spare time she keeps the apartment tidy."

Ulrike came the following day. It was quite amazing how she had blossomed in her early forties. Success was written all over her face. Her dress style reminded me of the young women in pre-Raphaelite paintings. She had carefully mapped out a future for her son which afforded her the freedom to absent herself as before.
When the tricky question of his real age arose, she smiled.
"Yes, I tried to pretend he was three years younger. Now, being wiser, I know how silly that was, nor did I fool

anyone. He is twenty-two years old and will move into a sheltered flat, specially equipped for people like him. The young men and women are mainly independent, meals are available in the dining-room for those who require them; the flats are cleaned. In the common room, the residents can socialize, make cups of tea and host parties. A warden is on call in case of need; transport is no problem as coaches are hired for the young students who live in the one-storey building; the gangways are wide and there is a lift. Hermann is so excited and ready to move in."

"You are not giving up your apartment, are you?"

"Oh no, whenever I am in London, he comes home for the weekend. Christine and I collect him and take him back on Sunday evening. I want to be near my son as much as possible, follow his progress; above all, be there for him."

It struck me that this last visit was by way of closure; she wanted to prove to me that after the death of her parents she had finally matured into a devoted mother.

But I was mistaken. Four years later I received a printed wedding invitation to the marriage of Christine Smith and Hermann Kütner, Bachelor of Arts. Underneath Ulrike had written: Junior Lecturer in English Literature.

Images on my Bedroom Walls

A web of memories spins around eight images on my bedroom walls.

1 Ashness Bridge

The bridge, covered in snow like the fells, reminds me of the years my fellow students and I spent in Keswick, Cumbria, where the Liverpool College had been relocated during WWII.

Evelyn and I used to wander up to Friars Crag to enjoy the finest views of the Lakes: looking north we saw Skiddaw, the mountain some of us had been foolish enough to climb in winter wearing town shoes. Surveying the scenery from this rocky promontory with John Ruskin's memorial, it was easy to appreciate that the 19th century Lake Poets were inspired by nature, motivating some to settle in the region.

Over ten years later my family made the Lake District our holiday destination. We drove to William Wordsworth's home. A housewife by then, I marvelled how his sister Dorothy, his constant companion even after his marriage and a poet in her own right, managed to cook in a kitchen without the electrical aids we take for granted, could also be so indispensable to her brother's success.

During spring the sight of the daffodils round the Lakes inspired Evelyn to recite Wordsworth's poem during our walks:

> "When all at once, I saw a crowd,
> A host of golden daffodils,

Beside the lake, beneath the trees,
Fluttering and dancing in the breeze..."

Seventy years have passed since our easy-going student days. Yet this poem "flashes upon my inward eye" as soon as I see tufts of daffodils in my garden. They remind me of our blithe student days.

We visited Beatrix Potter's farm near Sawrey Village, the backdrop of most of her twenty-three tales. The Tale of Peter Rabbit was one of our young daughter's favourites. As soon as she had spotted the figurines in the gift shops, she begged us to start a collection. We ended up with a total of 31 Beswick, Royal Albert and Doulton pieces; many of them are first editions.

Forward half a century, watched by his parents and myself, my grandson took them from the alcove in the sitting-room, downloaded them on e-Bay and Amazon on his mobile to ascertain the price of each porcelain item.

I had read the tales to him when he was a toddler; he used to caress each figurine. Now in his middle teens, the artistic value had lost its charm; the monetary worth was paramount.

* * *

The Lodore Hotel, Borrowdale Road, is one of my very special landmarks. I was a 'downstairs', live-in kitchen maid for ten days over Easter 1945 'to earn a crust'. (The pay, though welcome, was minimal.)

A decade later the former 'maid' had progressed 'upstairs', as one of the guests. Those rooms offered every comfort, sheer luxury compared to the sparsely furnished attic with unadorned white-washed walls. Along the narrow, uncarpeted corridor was the staff bathroom. The tub was encrusted with grime; when the coast was clear I used to creep to one of the guests' bathrooms to wash myself.

On holidays with my husband George and his mother, I learnt how the toffee-nosed county-set shunned strangers. They were wary of my mother-in-law who looked very foreign and spoke little English, viewing her from the corner of their eyes when she sat in the hotel lounge with her son after dinner.

He sensed she was not regarded as 'one of us': Alice 'displayed' herself in all her glory, unaware that the full-length black velvet dress, furs and jewellery round her neck and on her fingers did not fit in with the English upper-class dress-code of 'less being more'. What was suitable to wear in the Twenties in Berlin's theatrical circles was out of place in a hotel in North Wales. In vain George tried to encourage her to tone down the volume of her voice, wishing that the earth would swallow him up.

2 Water Lilies in Bodnant Gardens, North Wales

In 1951, while visiting my friend Evelyn, married to a Welshman, I discovered the valleys and mountains of North Wales. Many years later my family and I went back almost annually; we used to book rooms at the Royal Oak in Betws-y-Coed . The three-star hotel seemed adequate to my husband and me. It would have been considered sub-standard by Alice had she been with us.

She accompanied us only once. The most expensive hotel in the Italianate village, Port Meirion, designed by Sir William Clough-Ellis, had to be chosen. Then in his mid-eighties, he dressed smartly: grey plus-fours, knee-length white socks, a bow-tie round the collar of the white shirt, a waistcoat under his jacket with a decorative handkerchief in the top pocket. The grey hair, brushed back from his high brow, elongated the long face. He strutted around his domain, surveying with pride the architectural wonder he had created.

In that hotel history repeated itself with a vengeance. The upper-class guests examined 'the unwelcome intruders' and cold-shouldered us. Again Alice, having positioned herself in an easy-chair in all her finery, spread out the dark satin dress over her legs, adjusted the chinchilla cape over her shoulders and felt completely at ease. My husband and I could not hide our embarrassment.

Only our blond six-year-old daughter, poised daintily on a chair, her blue eyes trained on pieces of a puzzle in front of her, received the kind attention of an elderly gentleman. He sat down beside her and engaged her in conversation.

* * *

Over three decades later, George captured the beauty of a water-lily in middle of a lake at the Bodnant Gardens, a botanical garden, situated between Llanrwst and the coast. Like the flowers in Claude Monet's oil painting, it was in full bloom: long, pointed petals–red in the middle, edged in white–on a radial, green leaf.

For a little while we lingered, sharing a bench with another middle-aged couple. My gregarious husband chatted with them. There was much common ground. They, too, had served in WWII: he as a soldier, she as a nurse. The sight of maimed and dying servicemen and the suffering of innocent civilians had cast a lasting shadow over their lives.

I had not paid much attention to what I used to call 'war-talk', until I heard the wife's anguished cries.

"Never would I have dared to bring a child into a world, such as ours, exposing him or her to a future full of evil: intolerance, hatred and war."

With those words, she had dispelled the serenity of the surroundings.

We had always been positive and felt uncomfortable in their company. So we drove off towards the coastal resort of Rhos-on-Sea. Stepping into one of the seaside cafes, we were delighted to see almost as many cakes and pastries as in the Café Schuh in Interlaken, which we had patronised during our Swiss holidays.

The image of the water-lily conjures up precious memories of North Wales, landscapes in ever-changing light and shade, according to the trajectory of the sun, the clouds and the four seasons.

3 *La Parisienne*

'*La Parisienne*', almost as real as in a *tableau vivant*, is walking along *Les Champs Élisées* on a sunny day in mid-19th century Paris. Lady passengers are enjoying a ride in landaus drawn by horses; top-hatted men on horseback are just visible in the background.

In the foreground, her head tilted slightly, she views the onlooker with a smile on her lovely, carefully made-up, oval-shaped face. Black eyebrows and black lines with a hint of blue over the eye-lashes enhance her dark, liquid eyes. She has applied a touch of rouge on both cheeks of her cream-coloured skin. The slightly parted, well-shaped red lips seem ready to greet a friend.

La Parisienne, in her yellow bodice with a pink rose on the bust, a wasp waist and a bustle under the multi-coloured skirt, follows the fashion of the period. Long, frilled, white ruffles with a brown velvet ribbon and bow at the end of the narrow sleeves reveal a white-gloved hand. She presses a parasol to her side.

The face, crowned by a yellow straw bonnet and adorned with a nosegay of flowers, is tilted sideways towards the right. Her black, curly hair has been swept into the nape behind her ear, also covered by a nosegay; a diamond sparkles in the lobe.

Le jabot is fastened round her delicate neck with another dark brown ribbon and bow. *Le Jabot*, a word I first heard when I was a child, motivated me to look intently at the last family photograph taken in the summer of 1938, shortly before I went to Paris leaving my family behind.

That day my mother wore a *jabot* to brighten her dark blue dress. Later, in my aunt's *atelier de modes, la directrice* allowed me to copy in minute detail into a hard-backed black notebook the *jabots* she had designed.

The picture is signed S. Trevens. In search for information about him I browsed the net and downloaded paintings of 19th century beauties by John Lloyd Strevens. Was S. Trevens inspired by the Edwardian artist at a later date?

'La Parisienne' might have listened to the music in the *Tuileries* Gardens, as did Parisians in Eduard Manet's painting, dated 1862. Though it is less likely that a lady of high society would have mingled with the working-class, portrayed in Renoir's masterpiece, *Bal au Moulin de la Galette*, in 1876. We purchased a copy of this oil painting years ago; it hangs over the mantelpiece in my dining-room.

4 My Portrait

Vera, a gifted artist, my superior in the Parliamentary Committee on Refugees in the early Forties, presented us with the oil portrait shortly after our wedding day in March 1952.

The head and shoulders painting does not hide the imperfections of my face. My nose, according to my teacher in Nazi Germany over eighty years ago, is big but not considered curved enough to be classified as a Jewish nose. Due to my blue eyes and brown hair, I could have easily passed as an Aryan child.

Vera caught the amused expression in my face, with just a hint of a twinkle in my eyes. The head is tilted; sadly, the only comparison with *La Parisienne*. I had then (and still have) a boy's haircut: short back and sides; except in those days the fringe was parted on the right, it hides my lined brow now.

For the sitting we travelled to a village in Kent and walked to the annexe, converted into a studio flat, of an imposing property on her brother's estate. Former land-girls were working in the fields.

Vera took us to her mother's bungalow nearby. The old

lady in her mid-eighties, wearing a country suit, was living on her own. I marvelled at her courage and wondered whether I, should I reach such a great age, would be as self-sufficient as that tiny lady, a mother of four strong, tall offspring. Now, a nonagenarian, I have the answer. I am one of the many elderly widows in this area who has chosen not to abandon the marital home.

Before we left Vera, I gave her a photo my husband had taken, a glamorised version of his young wife, not the 'real me'. It does not reveal my 'real self' like this portrait.

During our short courtship of seven months, interrupted by a three-month visit to my brother in South America, he confessed that he had been attracted by my 'lovely legs' first of all; then by my interesting personality and intelligent face.

This portrait hung in our bedroom in my mother-in-law's Victorian property in Hampstead. Occasionally I gaze at it in the bedroom of my semi-detached house in Wembley which was bought in 1978. I notice how much my face has been exposed to the ravages of time - except for the blue eyes; they are still commented upon with flattering remarks.

5 Venice

During my childhood I was told that Venice was criss-crossed by canals and bridges. Ever since, the city has engaged my imagination vividly, transporting me into a magical world.

I discovered Canaletto's canvasses in the National Gallery, theatrical visions of his birthplace, in my late teens. He, like many other artists then, drew outlines of buildings with the aid of a *camera obscura* before starting to paint.

The famous city became the backdrop of Shakespeare's 'The Merchant of Venice'. I saw two performances, both equally memorable: Sir Laurence Olivier played Shylock clothed in Edwardian style, while Anthony Sher impersonated the role dressed in the garments worn by East European Jews living in the 16th century; the other actors in this production had put on period costumes.

Napoleon said that Venice was "the most beautiful drawing-room." The greatest English poets, including Byron, were lured to its shore. The city, reputed to be a den of iniquity between the 17th and 19th centuries, became a staging-post during the Grand Tour for the English nobility's sons and their acolytes. Far away from parental supervision they, like Casanova (the Italian adventurer), revelled in the depravity with total disregard for their aristocratic status.

At last I set foot in St. Mark's Square; nothing had prepared me for the impact *La Serenissima* made on me.
In the midst of a throng of tourists we followed the guide, listening to her tales about Venice's glorious past. She led us to magnificent churches and pointed out all the noteworthy architectural features of the splendid palaces lining the Grand Canal, inhabited by the nobility.
The Bridge of Sighs ("a palace and a prison on each hand" in Lord Byron's words) fascinated me the most. I imagined how the inquisitor's victims, aware of their dreaded fate, crossed from the Doge's Palace to the prison

cells in the claustrophobic atmosphere of the bridge and peered through the iron-barred, square windows for the last time.

As I examine this image, *laborati a mano* (hand-made) and painted in a V-shaped perspective, my eyes are drawn to the Bridge of Sighs. It straddles the canal between buildings in various shades of brown; a lone gondolier steers a black gondola with his long oar under the bridge. The Bridge of Sighs encapsulates my romantic recollections of Venice, a unique dream city.

6 Mont St. Michel

In July 1978 we downsized from my mother-in-law's fully detached Victorian property in West Hampstead to a semi-detached house in Wembley. The former charming, young owners needed to do likewise. They had to manage on one income due to the wife's pregnancy and moved to a cheaper area along the Metropolitan Line.

Before the end of the summer term, my husband, then a civil servant, used some of his accumulated weeks of paid leave to oversee the removal firm's employees. He watched them as they carefully packed, later unpacked, all our treasures and placed the furniture into the five rooms of our new home.

Due to the kindness of the couple who gave us access even before the deeds were signed, we were able to plan changes to the kitchen and order new units to be fitted as soon as we had settled in.

By the beginning of August, having acquainted ourselves

with the new neighbourhood and nearby supermarkets, we were ready to book a much-needed week's holiday; not too far away, just across the English Channel. However, we had left it so late that the choice of resorts and hotels was extremely limited.

Finally, the helpful local travel agent showed us a brochure of Mont St. Michel. This tempted us to risk staying in a one-star hotel in Brittany's coastal region.

We flew to Le Touquet. From there, a bus-ride of under half-an-hour took us to our destination. With difficulty, we lugged our cases and hold-alls to the hotel where a middle-aged woman welcomed *les anglais*, not very warmly, in her Breton accent. She was only used to 'native' tourists and apprehensive as to how we would fit into the jovial, noisy ambience during dinner-time.

When we entered the dining-room, she directed us to a table opposite the bar in order to keep an eye on us surreptitiously. Then she brought a large black bowl of mussels, a local delicacy we had never tasted before. All the diners behind us cracked open the shells, lifted them to the mouth; with the greatest gusto, speed and noise they slurped the slimy, brown substance inside them, as if their lives depended on it: not just half-a-dozen, but dozens. The empty shells landed in small buckets under the tables. We tried to hide our disgust. The irate *patron* cleared the full bowl away.

After that *Les anglais* did not endear themselves either because my husband complained, in bad French, that the wine had not been sufficiently chilled.

The accommodation in the attic proved to be another disaster. The double bed and cupboard filled our small

room. No doubt, the aqua-marine tiled bathroom en suite with a gleaming washbasin, *bidet* and toilet had earned the hotel a one-star status.
Sleep at night was impossible. The young couple in the next room were still 'performing' past midnight; yet in the morning they appeared fresh and rested at breakfast next for a *baguette* each with butter and black coffee.

Our teenage daughter fared far better. Her cubicle-like sleeping quarters were situated between two floors.
"*Où est la télévision?*" She enquired quite innocently after we had come downstairs again.
"*Pas de* television." *La patronne* informed her in a harsh voice.
"*Pas de television?*" Denise repeated in disbelief.

My spoilt better half had been accustomed to five-star hotels when on holiday in his youth. Even though he had slept under canvas while serving in the RAF during WWII, he grumbled about the lack of comfort every time he opened the door of our room.

I, for my part, had roughed it 'doing my bit' on the land, sharing a tent with another seventeen year old. I felt enriched by the experience of being among Bretons, so different from the people I had met in Paris and other parts of France.

The morning after our arrival was bathed in sunlight; even George had become his positive self again. Having decided on the spur of the moment to go to Mont St. Michel, we galloped to the bus stop as soon as we saw the vehicle in the distance.

It was low tide. Mont St. Michel, crowned by a statue of the saint, beckoned to us and other tourists who had also risen early. Inching nearer along the causeway, I was overwhelmed by the magnificent medieval gothic edifice, built on a rock of granite. We were shown the church and the great halls. From the 11th to the 16th century they had served as religious, military and civil centres. In the refectory of the monastery meals had been eaten in silence, while one of the monks, standing by a pulpit, read passages from The Holy Scriptures.

Before we left in the afternoon, we bought a copy of a painting, *Mont St. Michel la Nuit* (sold on Ebay for £31 plus £7.50 postage and packing), together with an illustrated guide. It is full of information about the architecture which had escaped our notice during our long sight-seeing tour.

The artist Maurice Legendre chose to paint the edifice at night. The façade is reflected in the water at high tide. Grey shadows obscure stores and fishermen's cottages outside the wall; only a few lamp-lit windows are bright.

From our hotel window we were unable to share the artist's vision of this unique place to which pilgrims used to flock for centuries. Yet, I was left with a lasting impression of Mont St. Michel, once described by Napoleon as 'The Wonder of the West'.

7 Die betende Hände (The praying hands)

Before I left my family in Frankfurt in August 1938 at the tender age of fourteen my father, a cultured man, had instilled in me an appreciation of literature and the theatre. During the open air *Römerberg* festival the previous summer, we had watched a production of Goethe's Faust Part I. The play was staged on the cobble-stoned area in front of the *Römer*, a medieval building which has been

Frankfurt's town hall for over six hundred years.

I still vividly recall Gretchen; her woes were incomprehensible to me. Lamenting the loss of her virginity, the maiden sat in her prison, like a bird in a cage. Nor could I grasp why Faust, a scholar, had signed a contract with Mephisto, the devil: his soul in exchange for her heart.

For many years I speculated why my father subjected his innocent daughter to this drama. Was it to shock me to such a degree that these particular scenes would stay with me for the rest of my life? Did he fear I might never have another chance to see Goethe's work performed in Germany in this historic place?

He proved to be right. After bomb damage during WWII much has been rebuilt. Alas, the words of famous classical German dramatists no longer echo on the *Römerberg*.

* * *

About seventy years ago, like other theatre 'buffs' whose funds were at a low ebb, I used to reserve one of the stools, lined up outside theatres in the West End of London, by placing a book, magazine or newspaper on it. This allowed me to walk away, return half-an-hour before the doors opened, certain that my property would not have been removed and get one of the cheapest, best seats. Oh, those were the days!

Meanwhile, I would wander through the West End to window-shop dresses or hats beyond my means, before treating myself to a meal at the 'Salad Bowl', in Lyon's Corner House in Tottenham Court Road for the sum of half-a-crown, 2s. 6d (old money), second helpings free. Afterwards, I strolled along Charing Cross Road to sort through the boxes full of old picture postcards on tables outside second-hand bookshops. As an adult I have had no compunction in handling old postcards or newsprint, though I have always refrained from acquiring books someone else has owned.

One of the postcards drew my attention: a copy of Albrecht Dürer's *Betende Hände*, hands drawn in pen and ink on a grey background. I remembered visiting the *Städel*, the 19th century art gallery in Frankfurt with my father. In one of the halls I must have seen some of artist's work for the first time. It occurred to me then how ignorant I was about all the great masterpieces and those who created them. To fill this gaping hole in my education I bought Kenneth Clarke's 'Civilisation' (a published version of the lecture series in the spring of 1969), at a much later date.

As a youngster, I read the titles embossed in gold on the spines of books, shelved in a book-case in the lounge; occasionally, I was even permitted to open the glass doors and take one of the precious old volumes in my hands.

In my father's bookshop I never ceased to wonder about the vast number of new books for sale and what had motivated the authors to write them. He pointed out to me that literature would provide me with a mine of information; it did during my student days–well before the world-wide web had been invented.

During my final year at primary school in Germany in 1933, before Jewish children were segregated in faith schools, my class teacher, Dr. Nickel, a paid-up member of the Nazi Party even before Hitler became chancellor and *au courant* with all the new racial laws, extolled the virtues of the Aryan race while pointing at the Swastika badge on his jacket's right lapel. Standing to attention in front of us, he declared, "WE, the pure Germans, belong to that superior race. Ours is 'the master race' of the world."

Ironically, as I discovered much later, orthodox Jews believe themselves to be 'the chosen people'!

I could not help thinking about what he had said so many decades ago when I looked at Dürer's 'Knight, Death and the Devil'. The knight, in Gothic armour, rides fearlessly to his destination, ignoring the devil's stare behind him and the skull lurking in the foreground.

If Dr. Nickel saw this image, he must have glowed with pride because the German artist endowed the work with the courageous German spirit. Yet Albrecht Dürer, born 1471, was not a typical German craftsman, although he was born in Nuremberg, the town of the infamous Nazi rallies. His father was Hungarian. Scrutinising a self-portrait for his 'Aryan' features, I detected none. With dark hair hanging in ringlets down to his shoulders, one must come to the conclusion that Dürer did not epitomize the 'pure' German.

'*Betende Hände*' was merely intended to be a sketch for an apostle's hands in one of Dürer's panel paintings. I was led to believe that these were his mother's hands, but read later that they were his own. Looking into a mirror, he drew his left hand. A second mirror duplicated the image optically, so that he was able to achieve the correct perspective.

Wherever I roamed I took the picture with me, even to South America in 1951. It reminds me to be humble and arouses in me a feeling of gratitude for what life has offered me during the past nine decades.

8 Baby Denise and her Oma (grandmother)

Her son's studio photograph portrays Oma supporting the two year old with one arm. The old lady is broad-shouldered in a grey silk dress, patterned with small black leaves. The pearls of her long necklace on her *décolleté* neck match those of her ear-rings. The hairdresser who used to visit her at home had rinsed the wavy grey hair light-blue.

The eyebrows, over hooded eyes, had been tinted black. A meaningful smile on her strong features reflects the essence of her domineering personality; it seems to announce, "I am, and will be, the mistress of my domain and of all who dwell in it."

A ball, almost twice the size of her head, is wedged in the infant's plump arms; grandmother looms behind her. With great interest Denise gazes attentively at her father, wondering why he is so intently looking into 'the black box'. She is quite unaware that her arrival would spark off such discord between three generations living under one roof.

Born in 1884, steeped in Victorian values, Oma intended to replicate the iron hold she had previously exercised on her much younger sister on her only grandchild. She was sure of herself. Being the head of the household, her volatile temper tended to be directed towards anyone who crossed her with a torrent of abuse, unconcerned as to who would hear her diatribe. The volume of her voice carried to the top of the two-storey house, as well as into the back garden where the little girl used to play. Frightened, she ran to me or to someone she trusted failing to understand why her daddy's mummy, who gave her so many presents, picked quarrels with every grown-up. These sudden outbursts alienated the bewildered grandchild she so passionately loved. She became bitter and resentful: it spoilt the rest of her life.

The manner in which my mother-in-law dealt with her nearest and dearest taught me not to be guided by her example. Once our daughter had grown up, been married and had become a mother, my motto has always been to give advice when asked and never ever to interfere or intrude into her family life.

From the day I met Alice until her death twenty-six years later, she failed to forge a close bond with all of us. I deeply regret that my daughter's grandmother was deprived of the happiness which I, Oma of a teenager, experience now.

Berlin

A couple of years after the Reunification of Germany in 1990 we flew to Berlin. The capital had been my husband's birthplace and the home of my maternal relations. We never went again. The four-day tour was action-packed. A coach drove us through East Berlin. We went to visit, on our own, Schloss-Charlottenburg, Schloss *Sans Soucis* and all the other places we had known during our youth.

We were struck that nothing much had changed on the Kurfüstendamm since 1938: certainly not the *Kaffeeleben* which we enjoyed that day immensely, while we watched prosperous, old boys chatting up *soi-disant* elegant ladies in their fading prime. In front of the Gedächtnisskirche, bomb-damaged during the war, a mime, clad in white, emulated the French actor Jean-Louis Barrault in *Les Enfants du Paradis*. His curved finger beckoned a keen amateur photographer and then, with a telling gesture of his hand, he demanded cash.

East Germans among the tourists looked with amazement at the luxury goods displayed in the famous store *das Kaufhaus des Westens* and in other shop windows. None of them could afford the prices. The *Mark* in the East had been devalued by two-thirds after the monetary union. Before, essential food and utility services had been subsidised by the Communist State.

My grandmother and one of my aunts, who had been unable to get out of Nazi Germany, lived in a block of flats in the Schlüterstrasse, a prosperous part of the capital. My parents moved in with them after the beginning of WWII. All were deported from flat no. 25. This and nearby buildings had been razed to the ground by Allied bombardment. The bombsite was a playground for immigrant children from Turkey.

My husband's former home had fared no better, but the corner bakery where he used to buy rolls as a child stood unharmed. We stepped inside the shop and refreshed ourselves with some coffee in the tea-room at the rear. The young lady who served came and sat down with us. She was the granddaughter of the owner my husband had known.

The synagogue in the Oranienburger Strasse, converted into the Jewish cultural centre and prayer-rooms, was guarded by police officers. That street had become an ethnic ghetto.

The following stories relate to two Berlin couples. The first we met in Germany after the Reunification; the second came to this country a few years before the Wall divided the Russian and Allied Sectors.

1 Resi and Werner

During that short break we visited the East German couple we had first met in a Black Forest resort during the previous summer. We, the only two foreign guests, had been encouraged by the proprietor of the hotel to share a table with them at meal-times. We introduced ourselves by explaining straightaway why we spoke German fluently.

"It is a privilege to meet you," said Werner. "We have never had a chance to talk with a former compatriot, nor have we ever been able to encounter a Jewish person."

"This puzzles me," I stated, "because I have known quite a few Jewish men and women, nearly all of them in their thirties (including a cousin of mine), who returned to the Russian Sector after the war with a mission to rebuild what had been destroyed by the Nazis and to re-educate the youth."

"Nobody took any notice of religious faiths." For a brief moment he hesitated. "I mean, after the war everyone was considered to be equal. Priests were no longer needed to teach people to love their neighbour."

Had Providence or some mysterious design engineered that we should cross paths with cultured people from Berlin so that they could throw light on the mind-set of their fellow-countrymen who had also chosen to remain in the East after the war was over? When we visited them, they provided the answer.

After retirement Resi and Werner moved to a small town east of the capital. They showed off their bungalow, one on a new estate; from their garden we could see the foundations for other houses.

Cakes, she had baked, and cups of loosened their tongues. I had the strong impression that they longed to talk to someone older than themselves about Germany during the Weimar Republic, a democracy, and the Third Reich, a dictatorship. They wanted to understand why and how everything changed after Hitler came to power in 1933.

His wife, more articulate than her husband, addressed us as follows, "We have learnt not to trust history books; all of them are biased. Truth has always been manipulated according to which side you are on. What really happened after Hitler became Germany's chancellor? How did the average German react to his new racial laws which had such a disastrous effect on the Jews?" She blushed, as she added, "We were only in our early teens; we were so confused." She intimated that they were too young to be blamed.

They had been born in 1923. Like all Aryan boys and girls growing up during the thirties and forties, they joined the Hitler Youth at a young age. (Group leaders were trained to indoctrinate the children in their charge.) Germans had been brain-washed by Nazi propaganda; no one dared to doubt Hitler's words in public.

On the polished oak sideboard stood a photo of young Werner, dressed in the uniform, though still in short trousers. I stared at it for several minutes. This made him feel uneasy.

"We had good times round the camp fire, just like the scouts, no different from the scouts," he mumbled.

Had my husband heard his remark, it would have alienated him. However, if sons and daughters had not joined Nazi organisations in those days, it would have aroused suspicion about their parents' allegiance to the Third Reich; everyone conformed. After the Allied victory, the Russians imposed their own version of dictatorship on all the conquered nations, including East Germany.

The couple's reaction to the Reunification after forty-five years took me by surprise.

"We were perfectly content," Werner stated. "There was full employment. The State was looking after us. One felt safe. Then everything changed. Officials from the West stripped any assets of value. State controlled enterprises and all their workers were taken over by private firms. This applied to us in the pharmaceutical industry. You were dismissed, if you did not fit into the new system."

He must have noticed our look of disbelief.

"We used to call the western intruders *'Besserwisser'*(know-alls). Nearly all of us, I mean our generation was content to sacrifice freedom of speech and press on the altar of security."

In a lighter vein Resi added, "Those in the West still regard us as second-class citizens and think we have nothing to contribute to the common good. Ah well, it's their loss, not ours."

2 Before Reunification

It was probably in 1956 when my mother-in-law engaged the couple from East Berlin. They were either sent by the Labour Exchange or introduced to her by a private employment agency.

The elderly residents, Jewish refugees from Central Europe, who spoke little or no English, were delighted that their needs were being understood, of greater importance to them at their age than the Germans' political views. With time on their hands, the inquisitive old age pensioners in her boarding house soon extracted personal details from both of them. Johann, he preferred to be called John, assured them "we have nothing to hide" and readily gave an account of their background, which the old folk 'chewed over' among themselves.

My husband and I, also in our early thirties, enjoyed their company after the evening meal, when they were off duty. We congregated round the cleaned kitchen table, hot cups of coffee in front of us, discussing what had happened in the past and how it had affected them and us.

We learnt that Ilse's and John's families had been close neighbours; the children had grown up together. Both sets of parents were wary of the National Socialists' propaganda spouted out by children's teachers and group leaders. They had always been Social Democrats. "Don't repeat outside what you hear at home," they were told over and over again.

John was called up when he reached military age. He kept his head down, held his own counsel throughout the long years of service abroad. On discharge he was lucky enough to return unharmed, eager to resume his studies.

Ilse, like all able-bodied women, was drafted into war work but had a chance to immerse herself in foreign classics with the help of her father, an English teacher.

After graduation and in full-time employment - Ilse had become a teacher, John a scientist - they married, setting up home in a one-room council flat in East Berlin. With enough money at their disposal, they believed everything they had ever wanted had come their way.

As soon as they had settled into a daily routine, they began to feel oppressed, most of all, when their parents talked about the freedom they had enjoyed during the Weimar Republic before Hitler's accession to power in 1933. In contact with their colleagues, both had to hide how much they hated living in the Russian sector under communist rule. They tried to swim with the flow.

"In the staff room the women teased me because I was still childless in my late twenties. The hatched-faced deputy head, a die-hard communist, even dared to ask me whether one of us sterile," Ilse told us. "She kept on reminding me that it was my duty to 'produce' strong boys to replace the men who had so bravely fought for the Fatherland. I prevaricated. After a while those of her ilk marginalised me, others grew tired of mocking me."

"We had made up our minds that we did not want to raise our children in a dictatorship," John continued. "So we applied for visas to go to the Western sector and, without our parents' blessing, we went to West Berlin. As a matter of fact there was an exodus of young valuable labour from East Germany until, of course, the soldiers on the look-out platforms of The Wall put a stop to it four years later. Most of the poor devils who tried to get away were shot!"

"And why didn't you remain in the West? After all, we know you received clearance from the American Occupation authorities and found well-paid jobs."

"That's correct. We were able to rent a bigger flat. Financially, we were much better off and money was available for research in the well-equipped new lab where I worked. We were certain that we had won *das grosse Los*. How do you say that in English?"

"We thought we had won the lottery," translated Ilse.

Impatient to reveal why their honey- moon with the West was short-lived, he continued, "The American way of life, as we saw it around us, distanced us from the people we met. We were put off by their noisy behaviour, their accent, the rowdy atmosphere in the dance halls. But they impressed the locals, especially the youth. They learnt how to jive, spoke with their accent and copied all the bad habits the GIs had brought with them. This led to confrontations with older relatives who were still traumatised by the recent past.

"So we finally made up our minds to come here, to London, where we hoped we could live the kind of quiet life we had known in our parental homes before the war," he concluded.

During the next few months we had fewer chances to chat together. Being pregnant, but still teaching, I needed more rest in the evenings and my husband, a free-lance photographer, kept irregular hours. Some time elapsed before we realised that something had changed in the couple's relationship. They used to go out arm-in-arm on Sundays, but they did not do it any more; nor did they exchange affectionate glances as they passed each other in the house. Meticulously they continued discharge their duties, though it became increasingly evident that their marriage was undergoing a great strain.

Finally John asked us in an a formal tone whether he and his wife could have a word with us that evening. We guessed what was coming.
"We regret to hand in a month's notice, or even longer if you are unable to find someone to replace us," Ilse began. "You have been good to us and we feel we owe you an explanation. We have decided to separate, not because we have met anyone else, but we have come to the conclusion that we do not love each other; perhaps we never did in an adult way."
I was quite shaken by this truthful admission and was just about to speak when she silenced me.
"Please hear me out; I also speak on John's behalf. We have been married for over ten years, been always on the move, never sure about where or when to have a child. But since we have been working as a pair, rarely apart, we have discovered that we have married far too young. First it was

the insecurity of not even knowing our 'real' place in the war-torn world; later, the struggle and excitement of finding what we believed would be our 'ideal' place held us together. We love this country, the kindness of the people, the friends we have made and have every intention to settle here, but by going our separate ways."

Neither of them volunteered any further information. True to their word, they stayed on until a replacement had been engaged.

Theirs was the fate of many couples either here or abroad who had been deprived to mature under normal circumstances into man- or womanhood before getting married. Those marriages lasted only a few years. It was less tragic when children were not involved.

Some divorcees remained single. A few friends of mine married again; they used to compare the first with their second husband, thus being unfair to their new partner.

The end of the war, the return of the soldiers and the so-called normalisation of one's existence brought many problems in its wake. Those of us who were not endowed with a survival kit went under.

My Three Sons

"Everyone has to reinvent himself," dictated Leena in a stern voice, once she had assembled the family. "I want MY sons to have the best education in England; to speak perfect English and mix with English students." Peering at Radi, her husband, from behind her glasses, she added firmly, "I have decided. We will relocate to London. Once there, I will reinvent myself too."

"What about my business? It's running so smoothly. Do we lack any comfort here, in Dhaka? The boys could be sent to boarding-schools in England."

"I am not parting with my sons. What sort of a mother do you think I am? Anyhow, this does not affect your business at all. Employ a manager and every so often make sure he does his job. Of course we will keep this house, and it will not cost YOU anything. With Eliza's help, I am going to find a suitable property and decide how I can invest some of the capital I have inherited from my late aunt. Rest assured, Radi, this is my own money," she stressed.

Unbeknown to him, she had worked it all out with her older cousin, Eliza, during frequent visits to London when the children were in the care of an efficient, trustworthy nanny. Later they discussed the move over the phone when no one else was in the house and via emails. As soon as she had read Eliza's, she deleted it. Between them, they had calculated the cost of an upheaval she deemed vital for the boys' future.

Radi, used to his wife's stubbornness, which invariably led to fundamental changes in his life, was trying to object in no uncertain terms. She forestalled him.

"Don't threaten to divorce me. You have no solid grounds," she snapped. "I am not for turning, like Mrs. Thatcher!"

At first, her three sons looked aghast at their mother. The very idea of 'reinventing' themselves fascinated them, though she had not been very explicit as to how this could be achieved.

"How are we supposed to do that?" Mushfiq, the eldest, asked.

"Easily done. As soon as we land on English soil you will be called 'George', Irfan 'Edward' and you, Samir, my youngest, 'Charles'."

"All names of English kings," cried 'Mr Show-off', Irfan. "Brilliant."

"And what could be more English than that," triumphed their mother.

At the beginning of the summer holidays the family flew to London and stayed at a West End hotel to orientate themselves. They were fluent English speakers with a slightest hint of a foreign accent, which the boys lost within the first six months.

Soon after their arrival an estate agent found a suitable, detached house in Eliza's pleasant neighbourhood. Leena was on 'over-drive' to get her family settled, while Radi had been detailed to look after the boys.

"Make sure you show them all the important historical monuments, apart from amusing yourselves."

She handed him a list of places in and outside London they should visit.

Her organisational skills were such that by the end of

August their new home, though not yet fully furnished, was ready for occupation. Charles had been enrolled into a local prep school; the other two were admitted to the public school at which Eliza's boy had started his 'A'-level course. Radi drove them to the schools for the first few days until they managed to get there without him, while his wife bought five semi-detached properties in the area, three of which had already been converted into flats.

"But what shall I do with myself all day?" she wondered when the deeds had been signed, as she walked through the local high street. It was then that she spotted a 'FOR SALE' sign fastened to an Indian restaurant. Without any hesitation, she started negotiations with the current owner in order to buy it.

Radi had not been consulted about any of her recent acquisitions, nor did she want his advice which would be negative. Facing him with the *fait accompli*, she told him, "I have waited long enough, frustrated, fearing I would end up as a mere housewife. Here I have reinvented myself as a modern woman. What about you? Why not set up a branch of your business in London?"

"No. I am not starting all over again. Three generations of my family have built up the thriving firm I inherited from my father. But I would consider a partnership in your restaurant. It would be a new start for me and at last we would be doing something together, as a couple."

She rejected his offer out of hand; an experienced manager had already been appointed.

"No. At last I can exercise my brain. Can't you understand that I am not one of those house-bound women who make an art of being housewives every morning and spend the afternoon in cafés, chatting about their uneventful lives with others like them?"

As they lay in bed at night, neither of them sleeping, he gently pushed his elbow into her side and sniggered, "I know you are awake. So just tell me, as you are so fond of reinvention, why haven't you adopted wearing European clothes?"

"In a sari I look different from other businesswomen, more attractive and feminine. This is a great asset when dealing with men."

Radi sank his head deep into the pillow next to a wife whose character he was only just beginning to comprehend after fourteen years of marriage. He realised he did not like London as a permanent home and made up his mind to return to Bangladesh for good. There, he would be considered a failure by their extended family for not keeping his wife under control. They would always ask, "When are they coming back?" or "Has Leena left you?" He could deal with that, but not with reinventing himself.

A French dictum, learnt long ago in school, sprang to his mind, *se sentir bien dans la peau*. "Yes, in Dhaka I feel comfortable in my skin. Why should I reinvent myself in a foreign country?" he whispered within Leena's earshot. She did not stir a muscle.

Next morning, while the family was still asleep, he packed his bags, crept downstairs and out of the house. She heard his footsteps but did not stop him.

"It's for the best," she thought and rehearsed how she would explain to the boys their father's sudden departure.

* * *

Four years later Eliza introduced Leena and George to me.

"I thank you for what you have done for my son," Eliza said. "In French he obtained an A*. As you lose him, you gain my friend's eldest. Can you fit him in?"

The boy's mother seemed very keen. The gangly youth looked non-committal, as if it did not concern him at all. With this pose he was hiding his shyness.

"Certainly," I replied. Addressing the youngster, I said, "It will be a pleasure. *Comment ça va? Bien?*"

He was blushing, tongue-tied, while Leena, upset by her son's awkwardness, sorted out dates and fees with me.

His siblings followed: Edward, more intelligent than the others, after two years; subsequently Charles, the liveliest of the three.

All of them were very bright, everyone in his own, unique fashion. George was extremely studious, painstaking and quiet. Only rarely would he mention his family.

Charles often lacked concentration. With his fertile imagination he sometimes managed to sidetrack me, until I pointed out that any conversations, unless in French, would have to wait until the lesson was over.

Edward, more articulate than his siblings, proved to be a difficult boy, presenting many problems to his mother. Their absentee father's sporadic presence had completely alienated them. During his brief stays he tried to impose his authority with a booming voice, always for wrong or trivial reasons. All of them were glad to see the back of him again.

Edward was past his fifteenth birthday when Leena rang me early one Sunday morning. This was quite unusual; the boy made his own way to my house and we were rarely in contact. The marks given to him by the French teacher for his work in school had been sufficient proof to her that her second son was on the right track.

"I need to see you urgently. I am at my wits' end. My son is suddenly turning into a Koran-reciting Muslim."

She waited to see what effect her news would have on me.

"You may be able to fathom out better than I do how his mind works. Please advise me how I can deal with this."

When I opened the door, I was taken aback: Leena looked so different without make-up in a brown trouser suit.

"There is just no one else to whom I can turn, not even my cousin. She is too impetuous. Eliza would call Edward a fool who was being brainwashed. She might cause more harm than good. You are an outsider, yet a person in whom he has put his trust. Being his teacher, you are able to reason with him rationally."

Her eyes begged me to listen to her confidence, but I doubted I could be of any assistance.

"Shortly before the end of our studies we were urged not to reveal either our political colour or our faith. I have abided by that sound principle for the whole of my career, especially when tutoring on a one-to-one basis."

"But Edward is being thoroughly misled by his friend's father, a devout Muslim, a neighbour of ours. He has urged my son only to respond to Irfan, his original Muslim name; to accompany him and his son Yusuf to the mosque on Fridays; to recite the prayers, and to insist on being transferred to the nearby Islamic school."

"This is just a phase. Teenagers are curious about the world around them."

"No, not at all. Yesterday he came back from next door full of the Holy Jihad with death to the Infidel; he wants to go back to his roots. My husband and I have been brought up in completely liberal families. I do not want him to be infected by the Imam's preaching. I have been told that he delivers his sermons in a measured voice, all the more powerful and dangerous as a result."

"How have the other two reacted?"

"George told him in his quiet way that he has stepped back into the past. Charles thought it was a huge joke, guffawing that our know-all is un-reinventing himself. But it's no joke."

"Dear Leena, you put me in an invidious position," I began, "especially in view of the conflict in the Middle East between Israelis and Palestinians; the death toll on both sides is rising. I am Jewish, but I blame them all alike, for not finding a peaceful solution."

"It is because you ARE Jewish and have witnessed as a child in Germany how hatred can destroy human life that you are best qualified to reason with Edward." Lowering her voice, she said, "Not only his but all our futures are at stake if he is exposed to that hardliner's destructive lectures for much longer."

"Radi? What does he think?"

"I have not told him. We are glad he is far away. He never needs to know. Hell would break out and drive the boy right into the Imam's arms."

Pastoral care had been of the greatest importance to me. I never turned away a student or parent who sought advice. I could not let Edward's distraught mother down. Therefore, after the next lesson with him, I raised her concerns for his spiritual well-being.

"Your mother came to see me last Sunday morning. She told me you are turning into a devout Muslim and that you go with your friend and his father to the mosque."

"Yes, that is true," he affirmed quietly. "There is next to

nothing I know about my faith. Neither my father, nor my mother has given us any guidance about the faith into which we were born. Yusuf's father is filling the gap."

His answer sounded plausible.

"That makes perfect sense to me," I assured him. "Every individual is entitled to learn about his roots; congregants should be able to worship in a mosque, temple, church or synagogue without fear and be inspired by the sermons. Unfortunately, and this applies to all religions, there are politically motivated preachers who tend to inject hatred and intolerance into their sermons."

He gazed at me intently as if I were analysing a complicated passage or phrase in a French text.

"Edward, I experienced as a child how intolerance changes into hatred and leads to the annihilation of millions only because they are of a minority faith or racial group, or because of the colour of their skin. Listening to the news bulletins, it is all being repeated today everywhere in the world.

"A charismatic teacher, rabbi, priest or imam is able to fan these deadly flames. I have witnessed how an average person can be persuaded to commit crimes against humanity; or to passively condone heinous acts; or, at best, to look away, pretending it does not concern him.

"Your history books teach you about the Inquisition. Innocent people were burnt alive if they refused to convert to Catholicism. During the Crusades, whole towns and villages were razed to the ground (causing the death of the people who lived in them), in the name of Christ, the Saviour, by knights from Europe. In the middle of the last century European Jews and those who resisted Hitler's dictatorial regime were deported in cattle trucks to ghettos in Poland and from there to death camps, such as Birkenau and Auschwitz. This was called the 'Final Solution' by the German Nazis who had planned it.

"I know for a fact that the horrors of the Holocaust form part of the history syllabus. Should your school arrange visits to the Holocaust Exhibition in the Imperial War Museum, you will see the replica models of the camps, their inmates and the collection of shoes, clothes and small possessions, once precious to their owners. Look at the ante-chamber in which the Jewish victims, including my own parents and members of my family, sat before they were forced naked into the gas chambers.

"On your way home, try to remember what I said to you just now. Edward, I beg you, think deeply about my childhood and early teenage story. It is a trauma which not only affected me but millions of others who perished. All was due to a populist orator and his rousing speeches to the masses; Hitler incited the hatred, which triggered human slaughter on an industrial scale."

I paused for a few seconds.

"I have talked for far too long, yet I count on you, a highly intelligent boy - no, you are nearly a young man," he blushed at my compliment, "to adopt my motto: Everyone is equal and should be treated with the same respect."

He shook my hand as he left. He had never done so before. I detected traces of tears in the corner of his eyes.

Shortly afterwards, Leena reported that Edward had severed all links with Yusuf and his family of his own free will. He pointedly refused to tell her why.

"Of course, I guessed it was you."

I was happy for her. It cemented our burgeoning friendship. We kept in regular touch.

Leena's three sons did well in the final exams; the eldest

gained 2 A*s, Edward 1 A*, 2 A's, while Charles, the scatterbrain, managed an A and 2 B's. Everyone was amazed at his results because his revision had been nil.

The boys rang to inform me of their future plans. Edward decided to study law. Subsequently he was taken on as a pupil at a firm of barristers at Lincoln's Inn. George enrolled in a postgraduate accountant's course. Charles, the *enfant terrible* according to his mother yet all the more likeable, toyed with grand scientific schemes but chose psychology, "Because I want to find out what makes us tick...and, most of all, what makes ME tick," he admitted.

* * *

At one of our frequent lunch engagements I was very pleased to see two of Leena's offspring. Although it was a Saturday, Edward was not in their company. His feeble excuse, relayed to me by his mother, was that he had to immerse himself in a complicated brief before appearing in Court. But halfway through the meal he did turn up after all.

"My son is the youngest practising barrister," Leena told me, her face shining with pride.

We spent a couple of hours in the most convivial atmosphere. The boys had not changed that much. George, 32 years old, was still introverted, listening rather than contributing to the conversation. He had not yet found his feet, sitting in front of the computer, applying unsuccessfully for a suitable position. Edward, just turned thirty and more voluble than before, talked enthusiastically about his career. He wanted to know whether the students I was tutoring were as clever as he was.

"The youngest is overweight and eats too many sweets.

He smokes, in spite of recurring asthma attacks," Leena sighed, back in a sari, not looking any older for the passage of time. "And he always orders the dessert richest in calories."

"I am celebrating our reunion! Ah well," he chuckled, "you only live once! Please excuse me. I am going outside. I need a puff."

He had spent a year in China where he did odd jobs and had loved it. Winking at his mother, "I am thinking of returning there one day. I might marry a Chinese girl."

"He is so rudderless," she winced, "and all of them still live at home."

"Not much longer. Next week I am off to Amsterdam. It's just a temporary position. The only qualification required is perfect English. It might lead to something permanent. On the other hand, I might choose a Dutch girl to be my wife."

* * *

"George's love life has been a disaster," Leena told me during our next meal together. "Did you notice that he hardly says anything? It's because he has been deeply hurt, not just once but twice, and struggles to come to terms with what has happened."

Then I heard the whole saga. Although he was still unable to earn his keep, Leena, with the best of intentions, introduced him to the daughter of a Bangladeshi acquaintance who, she hoped, would make a suitable wife. She sincerely believed as a married man he would not want to be beholden to his mother and her handouts. His new status would spur him on to find some employment and become his family's breadwinner.

Leena had another property converted into three flats, the penthouse for the young couple, the rest to be let. The bride's father bought the furniture and soft furnishings.

"It was like a little palace fit for a princess. I equipped the kitchen with all the labour-saving devices. The cupboards and drawers were full of expensive china dishes and silver cutlery.

"This was a big mistake I came to regret. The young wife mistook my generosity for a bottomless well from which she could finance her extravagant clothes. She was a spendthrift. George tried to remonstrate with her – all in vain. As soon as I refused to fund her frivolities any further unless she adopted a more sober attitude, her family was up in arms and sued for divorce on grounds of cruelty and incompatibility. George was no match for her on the witness stand. He was shy. His evidence was almost inaudible and confusing in spite of having been thoroughly briefed by our counsel and countless rehearsals of his testimony with his 'learned' brother at home.

"They won. I was landed with the cost. As for George, he was relieved to be rid of his wife, the cause of many rows between the two of us."

That same year Leena found another young Bangladeshi bride for George. On the rebound, he fell in love with her. A date for the betrothal was officially announced. She was delighted. At last her eldest would earn some money, due to the prospect of employment in the bride's father's firm.

But this fell through just one week before the wedding ceremony. According to a mutual friend of both families, his fiancée had been treated twice in a mental hospital. She was unbalanced, behaving capriciously.

"With me around, loving her," George insisted, "she

will be fine. I will take charge of any medication. Please, be happy for me. I know best."

His mother was unconvinced and asked Eliza via her grapevine, both in London and Dhaka, to make discreet enquiries about the family and in particular about the second daughter's health. She discovered that this was not the first time that the girl's marriage plans had to be aborted and tracked down the former bridegroom-to-be.

The young man came to see George and warned him not to go ahead.

"Honestly, it was pitiful to see her sliding away into a fantasy world. Only with professional care does she recover and no one can tell how long this will take or last."

Her son paid no heed to what he had been told. The date for the wedding was fixed.

"This is my destiny," he persisted eyeing his mother, "and a position is on offer. At last your eldest will be off your hands. That's what you have wanted, isn't it?"

The bride's father made extremely lavish arrangements in a five-star hotel and reserved suites for the guests who flew to London from Bangladesh. As part of the dowry he bought a bungalow with an extension for the young couple, had it redecorated and refurbished. As far as George was concerned, all augured well.

The bride's consultant had advised the mother always to check her daughter's medication and to ensure that she was taking all the required doses daily to ward off any new attacks during the weeks leading up to the festivities.

Unfortunately, she failed to do so. Her mind was too preoccupied concentrating on every minute detail, including the bride's and bridesmaids' dresses as well as her own attire, to make the occasion special, memorable. In the whirlpool of anticipation and excitement to which she was exposed in her home, the girl forgot to swallow the necessary pills and tablets. The inevitable happened two days prior to the wedding: she relapsed into a worse state than she had ever been before. There was no alternative; all the preparations had been in vain. The ceremony had to be called off.

"And you would not credit it. Her father instructed his solicitor that the deeds of the bungalow drawn up in favour of both in equal parts were to be annulled."

Leena pulled herself up to her full height, her voice booming across the restaurant. When she noticed people staring at her, she toned down the pitch of her voice to a whisper.

"Of course, they did not count on me, nor did they realize I had the upper hand. My son was fully entitled to keep the property by way of damages incurred, as he had been duped into this liaison; the mental history of the bride-to-be having been withheld from us.

"So, if it had not been for my intuition that what was proposed by her father sounded far too good, the poor boy would have had to endure another unpleasant divorce."

After careful consideration, the girl's father decided to settle out of court in view of the adverse repercussions it might have on his reputation as a businessman and an upstanding member of the Bangladeshi community. George sold the bungalow and gave the money to his mother in payment for the lawsuit he had lost. He had no desire to live in it; he wanted to erase her from his memory, a reminder of another failure within less than a year.

* * *

Leena's trials were not over yet.

"Sooner or later I will lose my sanity," she began, when we had ordered our meal a few weeks later.

"It is Charles's stupid flouting of the law which keeps me awake now. The easy-going, 'never-a-care in the world' son of mine is always short of cash and did not want to ask me again to pay for his fares into town. That is why, while Radi was in Dhaka, he helped himself to his father's Freedom Pass. He must have searched for it in all the jacket pockets until he found it in the heavy anorak which is hanging in the cupboard.

"In the station he inserted it into the barrier's ticket slot. It strikes me that he rather enjoyed this cat and mouse game, apart from saving money. Needless to report, his 'freedom trips' had been spotted. One morning he felt the heavy hand of a uniformed official on his shoulder.

"Young man, I have been watching you. You do not look like an old-age pensioner to me, more like a young man in his late twenties or early thirties who is attempting to defraud London Transport. You will be notified when you have to attend the hearing in court." After those few words he took down Charles's particulars."

Leena's greatest worry was not the hearing, but her husband's imminent arrival, which might coincide with the date. Again she had to rack her brain to think of a way to conceal their son's breach of the law without arousing his suspicion.

"As I told you before, he rages like a madman, makes all our lives unbearable. We begged our solicitor not to breathe a word of this to him. I seem to be tossed between the devil and the deep blue sea, and none of it of my making," she moaned.

Meanwhile her son gathered references from his friends, former teachers and lecturers; he appealed to me to write a testimony in his favour. We had a session together when I did so.

"It's like in the old days. I was always looking forward to the lessons, especially our chat afterwards...and I am not trying to butter you up," he finished with a smile.

I had a draft ready for him. He was pleased about my positive remarks but voiced his reservation about the final paragraph.

"Is it really wise to state, "It is the only blemish on his otherwise good character;   perhaps this offence should be considered with leniency"?"

"They respect a teacher who has watched you grow up into a fine teenager while tutoring your elder siblings. I sincerely believe my words will carry some weight."

After the hearing he rang.

"Today I am celebrating. I have only been cautioned by the judge. I am positive that your letter played a pivotal part. And I was so lucky that Dad did not find out."

* * *

At our usual haunt the waiters recognize us as soon as we enter the restaurant. After they had shown us, their faithful patrons, to a table, Leena spoke of Edward, THE son on whom she had pinned all her hopes.

"In a few words: he's fed up with the law in spite of winning so many law suits. He wants to study something else. "I'm bored with all the paraphernalia: the robes, the arcane ceremonies. Above all, I do not want to be a cog in the wheels of injustice."

"I had no idea what he was talking about. He explained

that "the honourable members of the bar defend clients with all the linguistic skills and gestures at their command and pick holes in their opposite number's arguments, whatever the truth of the case. We are paid to win."

"During the early years Edward treated it like a sport: two learned men fencing with words in a law court and the thrill after the punch that clinched the outcome. "I am haunted by the furious and sad faces of those who lost through my trickery," he told me.

"What on earth is wrong with all my sons? And there seems to be little progress in Edward's drawn out relationship with an English girl. It may even have come to a halt, not that he talks about it. Do I deserve this?"

"It will all blow over," I said and, changing the subject, I added "at least he pays for his board and lodging."

"No, he does not! All of them are living for FREE, like when they were children. He announced very clearly in front of the other two, "I'll pay for my board and lodging if the others do". "

Then she remembered that Charles actually had given her some money for three months.

"He worked for a charity, not a well-paid job. But at least he was earning a salary. None of his jobs last long. Guess why he quit?"

Her rhetorical question did not require an answer.

"He was outraged that the charitable organisation keeps too high a percentage of donations for overheads."

How typical of him, and endearing too, I thought. Not so in her eyes; so I kept *stumm*.

* * *

All the worries caused by her sons shrank into

insignificance after she got wind that Radi, her husband, was having an affair. It was Eliza, not the most sensitive person, who imparted the news to her after her return from Dhaka.

"He is not living on his own any more. If I were you, I would fly out *pronto*."

She did not breathe a word to the boys regarding the reason for her sudden departure, nor were they much concerned as their mother's movements were mostly unforeseeable.

Unannounced, as a rule they would confirm either her arrival in Dhaka or his in London a few days ahead, she unlocked the door of their marital home.

"Surprise, surprise," her tone was sharp but controlled, "a lovers' nest in my house!"

She glared at the young lady, less than half her age, as she sat with her red-faced husband.

"Your whore has the temerity to wear MY dressing-gown, probably share OUR bed with you, ousting me from my rightful place. How can you do this to me, your faithful wife and good mother to your sons?"

Her husband was lost for words. The young lady fled into the bedroom.

"This is the last straw. The boys and I have endured your volatile moods, your unreasonable demands and eccentricities long enough."

"Anyhow, I turned on my heels and took the first available plane back. He came to London a day later and accused me of being an absentee wife.

"After all, a man has his needs," was his excuse.

"It was HIS needs my egocentric husband was concerned about, not those of his family," she said to me afterwards bursting into bitter laughter. "I do not care about his needs any more. I wished him a long life with his present or another whore because I will not seek a divorce, as I have no intention of marrying again."

I could not help comparing my existence, always ordered and uncomplicated, with her turbulent life while she was driving me back to my house. She interrupted my thoughts.

"We selected the children's names according to their meanings and we found 'Radi' who is supposed to be 'satisfied'. Maybe it would have applied if I had proved to be a dutiful wife, rather than an anxious, doting mother.

Mushfiq/George, the eldest should be considerate. That he is when he is not overwhelmed by his past misfortunes. Samir/Charles, the youngest, is most entertaining; Irfan/Edward is supposed to be grateful for all the support given to him during his studies! Isn't it ironic that the only one who excels in his career now wants to opt out on moral grounds!"

She was more hopeful when we met again. Charles had been studying to become a qualified accountant, had slimmed down considerably to be more presentable and, even before the imminent final exam, was scanning the columns of financial papers for offers of employment, as well as being on the books of professional agencies. Edward was still at the bar. He was sensible enough not to make any rash, drastic decision. George was on campus and seemed to enjoy the company and studying again.

"But they still live with MOTHER. Yet there is hope on the horizon and, above all, we all get along peacefully without the constant fear of Radi's sudden arrival."

Carers

When I met Mala some twenty-five years ago, the word 'carer' had no meaning for me. She had 'clients': the misnomer describing the mentally challenged women who lived in her home. My admiration for her knew no bounds. Not only was this a full-time job, but also an invasion of her privacy. According to the directions from Social Services, her 'guests' were allowed to call her or go to her room whenever they felt in need.

Ann, the permanent client, IT 'guru' in spite of her disability, was awake during the night, visiting chat rooms, twitter and other social networks. Mala used to prepare a meal that could be put in the oven whenever she felt hungry. Yet when a sense of insecurity overwhelmed the sick woman, she would burst into her carer's bedroom for comfort.

Respite clients, who only stayed for brief periods in the absence of their permanent carer, provided a welcome additional income. There was little friction or contact between the two groups in Mala's care. Both tried to be on their best behaviour, striving to be praised like children.

* * *

My one hundred and five-year-old friend's carer lives in her house. I can- not help but notice how Feo couches her requests with utter politeness.

"Would you mind..." or "I would be much obliged if you could..." But the old lady's wishes are always carried out in a surly fashion.

I had been hoping I would never have to be in a similar position. However, *malheureusement* (unfortunately), my hopes were dashed over a year ago. It was obvious that I needed someone with me day and night after spinal surgery.

On my return home from hospital, Tahira, proprietress of a carers' agency, waited for me in the drive in front of my house. Near her stood a tall, slim Bangladeshi woman in a sari, a suitcase at her side. She looked bewildered at me with black eyes in an oval, dark face.

"This is Asha. She is well-versed in looking after old ladies like you," Tahira announced cheerfully.

I unlocked the door and ushered both inside, unsure of what I should make of my new companion. After a brief exchange between employer and employee, the two of us faced each other in the hall.

My husband had passed away three and a half years ago. It was a daunting prospect to have a complete stranger co-habiting with me. Exhausted as I was, I had to harness my mental and remaining physical strength in order to concentrate on how best to handle this new situation.

Asha followed me upstairs with her belongings. Once I had led her to the room she was to occupy, she assisted me with unpacking my suitcase. Eventually she appeared downstairs in her working clothes, a less attractive version of her previous attire.

In the small kitchen, I opened the various drawers and cupboards to familiarize her with the contents. As it was near my lunch-time (the dietician had advised that I should eat and take my medication at regular intervals), I put one of the frozen ready meals into the oven. The dessert had been prepared by my twice weekly help in advance.

In spite of following the instructions on the back of the cartons, it took us three days before we managed to heat a meal to the right temperature. This was not the only learning curve for the two of us.
Although Asha spoke English fluently, I seemed be the first European for whom she had to care. Her previous clients came from the Indian Sub-Continent. However, after many misunderstandings, we managed to 'rub along' fairly smoothly; though detecting an obstinate streak in her mindset, I tried to let her carry on the way she thought fit by giving her only the most necessary instructions.
She would have been a beautiful young woman with her regular features, if it had not been for her tense demeanour and at times sad expression, which she tried to hide.
"Chill out, girl," I wanted to say to the thirty-four year old, "you have a long life in front of you!"

Gradually I managed to walk a few steps in the garden and sit in one of the green chairs. Extremely alert to every one of my movements, lest I should fall and injure myself, she stood in the frame of the patio door ready to jump to my aid.
"Please draw up a chair, Asha. You deserve a rest after working so hard."
She placed the low garden table next to me and perched on it, keeping a vigilant eye.
"You have been with me now for over a week, young lady, and got to know me more intimately than my own daughter, but you have never told me anything about yourself," I said hesitantly, fearing a rebuff.
A smile spread slowly over her face and she began to relax.
"I share a little flat with my friend in East London. It's

not as nice as it is here. There is no garden and a lot of noise from neighbours, even late at night." And as an afterthought, as if it were of little importance, she whispered, "Oh yes, I have been married for a few years, no children."
"And your husband?"
"He is in Dhaka."
This answer did explain her long telephone calls at night on her mobile. That was all the information she volunteered. I did not want to pry any further.

"I appreciate the fact that so far you have not taken the two hours off per day, agreed as part of the arrangement. It just proves how conscientious you are. I am grateful to you for that."

Apart from the mandatory daily free time, she was allowed to absent herself for a day once a week. I suggested she should do so, forget about me and enjoy herself.

"Monday next I have a doctor's appointment I would like to keep. Is this all right with you? We will prepare your main meal as usual and I will tidy up everything before I go."

This she did conscientiously. As she closed the front door, she urged me to be especially careful since I would be on my own for the first time. It was quite a relief to be alone in the house, pleasing myself with no anxious eyes watching me continually. Nevertheless I had to admit that I was not really ready to manage adequately by myself. Although, the *modus operandi* of preparing a light supper far too early every afternoon, intimating "let's get it over as soon as possible", irritated me intensely. She never made a comment whenever I placed her carefully laid out food back in the fridge.

Dressed in one of her becoming traditional clothes, she reappeared shortly before seven o'clock. Her eyes were deeply red-rimmed, as if she had tried to rub them dry. She rushed upstairs. Except for checking I had taken my medication and seeing me into bed, she went to her room. Through the walls I heard her sob bitterly. I mulled over how and when I could find out what caused her such grief without being too intrusive.

The following afternoon, sitting in our usual places in the shade, I broached the questions which had haunted me before I had gone to sleep the previous night.

"Asha, did you have bad news from home? Are you unwell? What is wrong?"

She turned towards me, weighing me up. My concerned voice must have struck a chord with her strange, multi-layered mental make-up.

"I had to see a psychiatrist," she said under her breath.

"A shrink?" I mumbled like a fool, assessing the implications of such a consultation.

"No, not a shrink, a psychiatrist." Her tone was precise; 'shrink' was not in her vocabulary.

I was startled and alarmed. A 'carer', responsible for the general wellbeing of physically vulnerable old people, should not undergo treatment for neurological problems.

"I had another appointment with the psychiatrist," she snapped. I kept silent. We both remained so until, suddenly, with a complete mood-swing, the floodgates opened.

I have seen children cry because they have been hurt or thwarted and adults in mourning weep; but this was a deluge which would not stop. She shivered, even though it was a hot day. I was frightened I was witnessing the onset of an epileptic fit when she stretched out on the paved patio. There was no one around. My neighbours were out at work.

Instinctively I slightly lifted her head, put the cushion I had sat on under it and took her trembling hands into mine. It worked wonders: seeming to remind her that she was supposed to care for me, not I for her.

"I am so terribly sorry. Please, please don't speak about this to the agency. Believe me, I am fond of old people and I need this job," she implored me.

"We will keep it between ourselves, if you are completely honest with me about your state of health in the future."

"I have seen the consultant once before. Yesterday he wanted to know if the tranquillisers he prescribed are curing me of depression."

Again I was stunned. A depressive was in charge of a nonagenarian who needed care!

"It's all about the lovely old lady, my lovely old lady." After a long pause, she said, "She died while I was alone with her. Alone, quite alone."

There was another eruption of tears. She managed to stifle them.

"I loved her, like I do my grand- mother... such a good woman, the first person who has ever really understood me in this country," she cried out.

Clutching my walking-stick with one hand I led her inside with the other, made her sit down and brewed tea, which I wheeled in on a trolley. Gradually she calmed down. Even earlier than usual, she prepared the sandwiches that I would eat in the evening. I let it go.

During the following week she addressed me only when absolutely necessary, keeping her inner self veiled in darkness. Otherwise she carried out her duties in silence. She no longer joined me for a chat in the garden. Most probably she regretted treating me as a friend, not as a stranger. Also, she may have been worried I might decide to send a negative report to the agency after all.

Asha's unexpected *volte face* was surprising to say the least during her last morning with me. She assisted me in getting ready for the day almost tenderly.

At nine o'clock the employment agent called with her replacement.

Taking great pains, Asha showed the middle-aged, much more experienced carer around the house and enumerated what was expected of her.

"Your new client is waiting for us, Asha," she was reminded. But instead of joining Tahira straight away, she went into the sitting-room and wrote her mobile number into my address book with an asterisk at the side.

"Please call me when you need me. I enjoyed so much being with you."

As the door closed on them and I heard them drive away, I pondered about Asha's paradoxical nature and questioned whether she was mentally adequately equipped to shoulder the responsibilities of a 'carer'!

A Teachers Reunion

It was the first time for nine years in 1987 since I had stepped out of West Hampstead Station once again. I felt alienated in the area where I had lived for over three decades. The delicatessen opposite, where my mother-in-law had quarrelled and made peace with the Jewish owner several times over trifling matters, is now a housing centre. The Acol Bridge Club along West End Lane, which my Japanese neighbour in North Wembley patronises, was in full swing. A new Czech restaurant in one of the old Victorian houses attracted my attention. The distance between Linda's flat in Cleve Road and my former home in Hemstal Road until 1978, had seemed far shorter according to my mental street plan.

I had never been inside that old-fashioned, gloomy block of flats before. The lift, hard to open and shut, was no more modern than the one in Foyles bookshop in Charing Cross Road in the late 1940s.

On the third floor, flat no. 22, Linda wafted out of the front door in a russet shirt and a flowing, colourful, narrowly pleated midi-length skirt, as dictated by fashion. She welcomed me effusively; then led me into the square hall with a cupboard for cloaks–the French would say *'grand comme un mouchoir'* (as big as a handkerchief) with the *bijou* kitchen opposite.

Two vaguely familiar male voices seeped from the sitting-cum-dining room. Ian, looking aged, the face slightly fuller, his hair grey and in casual dress, was in deep conversation with Alex. He had not changed at all, nor had his apparel: a grey, badly fitting suit and white trainers.

The room gave onto a long, narrow corridor. On the left, the small bedroom reminded me of a French lady's *boudoir*; the master bedroom with a window from floor to ceiling accommodated guests. A bathroom with toilet and bidet was at the far end of the corridor, decorated in light green.

On the glass shelves over the washbasin the scent emanating from an array of bottles and tubes almost overpowered me. While I was on my own, I was bitchy enough to scan every corner to detect some evidence of a 'lodger' because Linda, in her late forties, was still "collecting male companions from the street," unkind mouths were whispering.

Even her 'best friend' and colleague, Samantha, once referred to a young Israeli who, Linda had told her, had lost his way in front of the building and had nowhere to go. Out of the goodness of her heart she offered him shelter, warmth and her company for the night in the master bedroom. That a young man had dashed out of the flat just as Samantha got out of the lift. However, I gave little credence to the many half-truths told in the staff room by other teachers.

Back in sitting room, I sank into the blue, patterned armchair next to Alex. It was far too high for my short legs and too soft for my back.

Ian was talking about coaching students on a private basis. Apparently, the going rate was £15 - £30. He turned towards me, claiming, "The more you charge, the better they think you are. And where do you find your young candidates? Through an agency or do you advertise in the local press?"

He was seriously interested, but left after he had heard

that apart from teaching I was also publicising the English version of my German autobiography and writing short stories.

Alex noted the title of my book on a scrap of paper he had fished out of his jacket pocket. I thanked him for the Christmas cards he had sent me every year and asked him to give me his present address. He had it ready for me in large, straight letters on a stamped envelope.

"I am really sorry I did not keep in touch. Why did you not ring me?"

"I do not want to talk about it. It's water under the bridge!"

He wiped his eyes until they were red.

Val entered the room. We both had retired at the end of that summer term. She had just turned sixty; I had remained in my post until a few days before my sixty-fourth birthday. Her hairstyle was still the same: short, a parting at the left side, now with a few grey strands in her pitch-black hair. She wore a becoming dress and red shoes of the latest fashion–so unlike the way she looked in the dreary dark outfits many years ago. Chris, her companion, probably her lover, a tall man with a pleasant personality who, she remarked, had almost regained the use of his hands after a stroke, came in with her.

She planted herself next to me and put a photo album into my lap.

"Our little retreat in Brittany, the tumble-down property we bought is now almost in pristine order. We spend the summer there and invite our town-weary friends to join us. The locals have been most welcoming in this beautiful part of France–not yet overrun by Ex-pats. The rest of the year we live in London. I intend to find a larger pad somewhere in Maida Vale."

I responded to her news by showing her recent photos of my daughter and her husband, telling her that Denise still uses her maiden name in business.

"And quite rightly so," she agreed. "Why on earth should a woman have to adopt her husband's surname?"

I remembered how bellicose a colleague she had been and how I always tried to stay clear of her in the staff room because some of her 'feminist' notions were nonsensical. Some colleagues, spinsters like her but less obsessed about women's rights and bored by their dull existence once the school day was over, used to argue with her until the sound of the bell called us back into the classroom. It further occurred to me that on a class teacher's pitiful pension she could hardly have afforded a holiday cottage abroad and 'a pad' in an up-market residential area in London. A 'true feminist' would be independent and not be beholden to an affluent male, whatever role he played in their relationship.

Margaret, also in her early sixties, arrived later with a big bunch of flowers. She wore an expensive, loose, elegant jacket to cover up her balloon-like figure, hiding the weight she had put on. She luxuriates in her newly found freedom, but did not tell us how she spends the time. Her blond, curly hair had strands of grey with a fringe to cover the deep grooves in her brow. She, a Catholic, still lived with Eddie, a successful entrepreneur, in a maisonette nearby. They married some years ago after his mother, who would not tolerate 'a gentile' in her Jewish family, had passed away.

The sandwiches and pastries were so rich in calories that I did not eat anything. This gave me the chance to watch my former colleagues; they tucked into everything. Val and Margaret, built like Wagner's *Rheintöchter* (Rhinemaidens), consumed more than was good for them.

"My lunch was very frugal today," the latter warbled, "because I knew our hostess would spoil us at teatime."

Linda, soon to be retired, observed, "Helga, you had a knack of keeping the pupils quiet. Our intake has shrunk so dramatically that there is talk about amalgamation with John Keats next door. In the meantime, they are looking for another deputy head for the senior department, as Peter will join the retired brigade. Someone had heard from Brenda. She had become a globetrotter, but could only write with a pencil, due to her arthritic hands. But Sue, Christine and Elizabeth are still toiling away."

While they were rattling on, I realized that the 'inner circle' to which I had never belonged still kept in close touch. Their body language and innuendos made me feel I was an outsider, like Alex.

We left before the others. In his shy manner, he doled out booklets about Chartres and Paris, still in my possession after all these years. As we parted I promised to invite him–a promise I have never kept.

'Beware of Intruders'

Before, during and after WWII, we used to leave the backdoor ajar all day and the milk money under the empty bottles, in the certainty that no intruder or passer-by would steal the cash. It is so hard for us who have grown up during those decades to come to grips with the fact that now you cannot trust strangers.

1 The Window Cleaner

The front door bell rang on a bright Easter Sunday morning.

"I've come to clean your windows, madam."

"But it's Easter Sunday?"

"Yes, I even have to work today to feed my family. As I am in this area, I can fit you in."

"No, thank you. I have had the same window cleaner for over twenty years and I have no reason to change."

I closed the door on the tall, white man in his mid-thirties, his blond hair cut like a soldier's, with an educated English accent and an engaging expression. He was dressed in clean jeans, open-neck white shirt with a black leather jacket slung over his right shoulder–unlike the run-of-the-mill window cleaner who was working for me.

Completely forgetting his existence and the sliding door of the sitting room I had left ajar, I returned to the painstaking task of correcting, more than I cared to count, the mistakes of my manuscript, recently sent back by the proof reader.

Footsteps on the squeaking stairs aroused my suspicion; we had not got round to having them repaired. The self-professed window cleaner, without the tools of his trade, was slowly descending to the bottom.

"I told you that I did not need your services. I did not want you to come into my house," I shouted up at him.

"You owe me £10 for what I have done so far," he said grimly; unspoken threats darted from his eyes.

Not daunted by the seriousness of the situation, (the man could have easily knocked down my fragile, short frame in one blow) I refused to pay for unwanted services.

"I am calling the police this instant as well as my neighbours, all of them strong fellows."

"No, don't do that! I am waiving my fees. I will leave straight away."

He got out through the open patio door and rushed to the garden gate, which was anything but secure.

The neighbours came straight away; the police after five minutes. Finger prints were taken. No match. The police van cruised round the area. The man had vanished into thin air.

Now the garden gate is barred with bolts, locked with a padlock and, above all, I have learned an important lesson: never, ever leave any of the three doors into the house open.

2 Loft Insulation Reps

It was pitch-black and cold that Friday night. The shrill sound of the door bell rang through the house.

Wary of another intruder, I reluctantly unlocked the inner door, adjusted the security chain on the porch door, switched on the light and looked through the open slit.

Two girls in their twenties stood outside, their faces eerily lit by the street lamp.

"Are you the owner of this house?" asked the taller one

with a very strong Polish accent.

"Who wants to know?"

"We came to measure the thickness of your loft insulation," and with that she tried, unsuccessfully, to put a foot in the entrance.

"Not now! If you like, come back in the morning," I replied, easing her foot out of the way and locked up again. However, their shadowy outlines did not move. The bell was rung with great urgency.

"It's free. You don't need to pay," one of them screamed.

Straight away I ignored their enticing offer. Eventually they went, accompanied by a man who had been lurking in the background.

Next morning one of them reappeared, clutching a tape measure. To prove her credentials a badge was pinned to her duffle-coat.

"You have had a wasted journey. Sorry, I do not let strangers into my house. By the way, you are just touting for business for your employer's firm, aren't you?"

"I do not understand."

"You are Polish. What is the name of the firm?"

"Mila and Patisen. The loft isolation is free," she stressed.

"Mila and Patisen. I have never heard of them."

I looked closely at her identification badge. I read, 'Miller and Patterson Sheffield'.

"Look, I won't detain you any longer. I am going to consult my builder for his advice."

This time she got the message.

"Loft insulation for free," I enthused and picked up the

receiver to ring the local council. After pressing several buttons and listening to repetitive musical entertainment for nearly ten minutes, I actually heard a human voice.

"How can I help you," the advisor enquired after he had checked my personal details.

I stated my request and, indeed, I qualified for a grant to insulate the loft. But there was a snag: as there was a backlog of applications mine would not be dealt with until February at the earliest. I protested, stating that being a nonagenarian, I was suffering miserably during the winter months. Furthermore, he then added, the work would be carried out by the council's contractors.

"I don't let complete strangers into my house. Can I not ask my builder who has been looking after my property for over thirty years?"

The advisor's reply was short and negative. "Only the council's contractors can carry out the work."

So I drew a complete blank. I could not wait another three months for house improvements which would help to keep me warm. And the very idea of strangers running up and down the stairs after my experience with the first intruder sent even more shivers down my spine.

3 The Tree Surgeons

This unfortunate episode occurred while my husband was still alive, although already a very sick man.

"That tree needs cutting down. The branches are hanging over the fence. It's against the by-laws," the hefty, ginger-haired man at the front door explained in a husky voice.

We looked at his dilapidated van.
"What is your price?"
"Only fifty quid."
My husband turned towards me. I nodded.
"Just this tree, not the other one, at £50," he emphasized.

A second man opened the back of the van and, to our horror, two street urchins, looking like mischievous imps, climbed out as well, and ran around us as we tried to get back into the house. They followed close on our heels.

The older one prodded me in the back. With his head tilted upwards he leered at me with half-closed eyes, hissing like a poisonous snake.

I was terrified when he tried to get into the room at the back of the house with his brother. With a bang I shut the patio door and bolted it. They pressed their faces to the glass and made devilish grimaces, hooting and laughing.

My husband was surveying the men at work from an upstairs window.

"Not the other tree," he shrieked, running downstairs out into the garden through the unlocked kitchen door.

The men had butchered the tree which had to be cut down by a *bona fide* tree surgeon. A loud argument between my husband and one of them ensued, my spouse looking diminutive in his presence.

Meanwhile, the two little fiends moved swiftly towards the door, which he had left ajar. I beat them to it and secured it from outside just in the nick of time.

One of the two men lifted his arm ready to strike my over-excited spouse. At that moment, I seriously feared for our safety; the two boys took in the scene in order to learn from their elders.

At least they were not making an unholy racket any more and stood still. Misguidedly, I asked them why they were not at school.

Their reply, laced with a string of swear words, was too rude to be put on paper.

As my angina-suffering octogenarian spouse was getting nowhere and possibly inducing a heart attack, I stepped in. I realised that by the time I had rung the police and awaited their arrival, one or both of us could have been severely harmed.

"If you leave our premises, take the children into the van and stay put outside the front door, I will give you the money: £50 for the tree, which according to you has been professionally cut, and another £50 for never coming back again."

With greedy fingers they accepted the cash, gathered their brood, pushed them unceremoniously into the van, got in themselves and set off at great speed.

I thought my solution had been inspired by the wisdom of Solomon: no price was too high for the sake of peace. However my husband was underwhelmed and chided me for what he felt was the unnecessary loss of money.

3 The Builders

The door bell rang. Following the advice of a solicitous friend, I fastened the safety chain on the front door before opening it. A young, ginger-haired man in workman's clothes faced me.

"Have you heard the weather forecast? Severe storms are moving this way. I looked across after I had checked your neighbour's roof and noticed a couple of tiles have slipped into the gutter. I can fix them for you, it won't take a minute."

"No, thank you. I will ring my builder who has been looking after us for many years."

"Oh, you don't need to bother him. It's such a small job and I have my ladders here," he said, smiling down at me. "And as you are such a nice, old lady I can do it for you for £5."

Once again, I had been caught off guard by the persuasive manner of the caller, so I nodded.

"All right then. I'll be back in a jiffy!"

"Wait," I called after him. "I am not opening the garden gate. Please pull up a slat of the fence to let yourself into the back garden."

Less than five minutes later he reappeared with an older burly type who carried a ladder and a grey, dirty bucket filled with big chunks of mortar.

"See this mortar? That's come off your roof. All your rib tiles need to be fixed into place. We can do it straight away for £100 in cash."

Even with my little knowledge of rib tiles, I knew that they were held together by a thin layer of mortar. The penny had dropped with a loud bang in my brain. "Will I ever learn?" I muttered under my breath.

"Beg your pardon, madam. I didn't quite catch what you said. Shall we go ahead?"

"Do you think an OAP can afford such a big sum?"

He moved his lips, calculating the cost of material and work.

"Ah well, let's say £50 in ready cash and we'll get what we need from the builders yard."

"I am very sorry to disappoint you, but I never keep much cash in the house, certainly not as much as £50."

The pleasant smile, which had lit up his face before, vanished.

"How much then?" he snapped.

"£20."

"That'll have to do then," he snarled.

"Please wait."

I locked the kitchen door and switched on the alarm, increasingly worried about the harm they could inflict on my person and the damage they could do to the roof. However, years of teaching experience had taught me never to betray my emotions, even in perilous situations such as this one.

With a nonchalant expression I handed the young man twenty pounds and asked him to let himself and his colleague out the way they had come in and push the slat of the fence down afterwards.

He pocketed the money and signalled to the other man, who seemed to be quite inarticulate, to follow him across the garden to the gap in the fence. They stepped into the road and pushed down the slat.

As soon as the coast was clear, I looked up at the roof at the back and in front to make sure that the rib tiles had not been tampered with. But it needed the expert eye of my builder to carefully check the roof.

What a relief it was to be reassured, once again, by my long-suffering builder, that the tiles and rib-tiles were all intact.

The Matchmaker

Ever since seeing 'Fiddler on the Roof' with Chaim Topol as Tevje when it was released in this country in 1971, one of several film versions of Sholem Aleichem's story published in Yiddish in 1894, I have been intrigued by the role of the *Shadchan/Schadchen* (matchmaker) who played a pivotal role in finding prospective partners for eligible sons and daughters. She would gather financial and personal information about her client's family, leaf through her filing index (probably now download details from the internet), to find the most suitable match.

If she was successful, both parents would be invited to discuss all relevant issues, including the bride's dowry. Only once everything had been sorted out would the young people meet each other. Should there be no common ground between them, they would not be coerced by either side to go ahead. In that case, the matchmaker would return to her 'drawing board' and try again.

* * *

In Poland and Russia up to the First World War Jews, fearing persecution and progroms (the organised massacre of Jews, originally in Russia), lived in *shtetls* (small communities) outside the villages of their Christian neighbours. Contact between them, during rare peaceful periods, was only on a commercial basis. Socially both groups lived completely different lives.

It was a revelation to me when I found out that in the 21st Century this tradition is still observed in ultra-orthodox communities, though even I, (a modern young woman in 1951 who had only gone out with what in German is called *linke Füsse*, left-footers considered unsuitable candidates) was introduced to my future husband by a German Jewish friend from Frankfurt: acting like a latter-day *Schadchen*.

* * *

Fast forward to the summer of 1983, to the Bernese *Oberland*! The three of us, father, mother and daughter were sitting opposite another set of parents, their offspring a son in his forties, in the compartment of a funicular (cable mountain railway), which was ferrying us from Interlaken to the *Jungfraujoch* Station.

His mother quite unashamedly was inspecting our extremely attractive twenty-six-year-old daughter from head to foot, as if she wanted to take stock of every inch of her persona. It was so embarrassing that Denise, dressed in a blue tee-shirt and denim trousers, turned her blushing face to the window. We guessed straight away that the woman, a typical *Yiddishe mamma* from the Bronx in New York, was in match-making mode. In those circles it was considered proper that a man should be established professionally, be married by the age of thirty-five and have fathered at least two children.

The lack of her son's drive and inertia had become such an obsession with her that she desperately searched for a future partner on his behalf, even on such a glorious morning with the dramatic Alpine landscape spread out before us, as we moved ever higher up the mountain slope.

The funicular was due to pass through the tunnels of the Eiger and Mönch mountains. Tourists were allowed to get out of the carriages at the Eiger Station for five minutes to look at the mountain face and at the second stop to see the *Eismeer* (sea of ice) sparkling in the sunshine.

If my memory does not deceive me after more than three decades, the journey lasted almost two-and-a-half hours. It needed adroit handling during that time to win our daughter's attention and possible interest in the match the son's mother was about to propose. The impact and flow of her persuasive words aimed at us were to draw our attention away from nature's wonders.

She set to work super-fast.

"May I introduce myself," and despite our obvious impassivity, she continued nevertheless, pointing to her two male companions, "This is Joseph Goldberg, my husband, and this is Jonathan, our son."

The two men bowed.

"We have never been in Switzerland before. It's all so exciting. The clean air, the cloudless sky, the mountains," she gushed. "We have been in Europe before–to Russia, where our grandparents were born. Their children left for America with an uncle soon after their *Bar Mitzba* (Jewish boys are confirmed at their 13th birthday), to get away from the progroms. Both became American citizens; one of them was my father who passed away ten years ago."

Assuming quite rightly that we, too, were Jewish, she expected us to provide a short résumé of our antecedents. As we did not oblige, she targeted our daughter with a barrage of personal questions: her age, likes, dislikes, hobbies and profession. In German such a frontal attack was termed *Hals und Kragenweite* (neck and collar size), which we all agreed afterwards was unwelcome and rude.

Denise's answers were as brief as possible. At one point my husband wanted to abort the 'interrogation', but he refrained from doing so.

"I expect you are still single, coming on holidays with your parents. So is our son, not a high flyer like you, young lady. He is a psychiatric nurse, utterly devoted to his patients. So he never has any time to find a wife. But you can explain what your duties are so much better than I can," she urged him on.

The three of us felt sorry for the guy, his face as red as a beetroot. He had been hoping to relax away from his mentally and physically demanding job during the holidays. But he did not want to upset his well-meaning mother.

"I have grown extremely fond of the young people under my care and I think they trust me. The majority of them have had to submit to maltreatment by their own parents who were unable to cope with their mentally deficient offspring. That is why they are never quite sure of other people's intentions, nor do they have any confidence in their own judgment. I am a kind of warden in their home. After fifteen years of service I am due to be promoted on my return to a different job and am free to rent a flat."

"Yes," his mother announced excitedly, "My son, Inspector Jonathan Goldberg, does not need to live with the mad hatters any more..."

"Mother, don't call them that. They are human beings like you and me and entitled to be respected."

"Oh whatever," she hissed through her ill-fitting teeth. "Jonathan's salary is going to increase considerably. With normal working hours from 9 am to 5 pm, as well as weekends free, he will at last have time to find a wife–at forty-two!" She spat out the last three words like an insult.

Neither Jonathan nor his father could conceal their shame about the manner in which she talked to us about her son's future.

"He's always been a good boy ever since his youth. He is thoughtful and kind. He wouldn't hurt a fly. There are not many like him left in this modern age. He is someone who will give, never take," she stressed, mainly addressing our daughter.

And in a plaintive, dramatic voice, she pressed on, "Before, he didn't have enough time to mix with other young people and now, when he has, he is too shy to even approach one of the young ladies in our synagogue's congregation," and to everyone's disgust, she concluded, "so, I see it as a mother's duty to find him a wife."

Sheer providence would have it that we had just reached the *Eigerwand*. As soon as we could, we got out of the compartment. She tried to follow us but her husband stopped her.

Had there been some free places on the train, we would have changed seats. There were none; we had no choice but to return to them. On their faces we could read that the family had had a blistering row during our short absence.

As we entered the carriage, Jonathan looked straight at our daughter. He had been press-ganged by his irate mother to make a move.

"Have you ever been to Chicago? I expect you have been to New York - all English people only visit New York, but Chicago can also offer many attractions. I would be happy to show you round," he said in a pleasant voice.

Our daughter, not usually short of words, did not respond.

"Oh there is no obligation whatsoever. Please ignore what my mother said. She is just eager to see me settled, apart from the fact that she, like her friends, could rant on about an awful daughter-in-law and her dreadful parents."

She was pleased that he finally communicated, although it was not quite what she had expected.

Denise felt this was the right moment to end the absurd charade.

"True, I travel on business, but never to Chicago." To make sure her message hit home, she said, "I do not intend to get married yet, especially away from my parents and friends."

We had reached the Sea of Ice and got out once more. On our return, both mother and son, duly chastened by the father, remained silent until we reached the *Jungfraujoch*.

The three of us left the terminus and breathed in the fresh air. Later on we found a table at the far end of the cafeteria to avoid any further contact. We did not see them afterwards. If we had, I would have taken her aside and advised her to leave it to a professional matchmaker, as she was definitely unsuited to take on the role herself.

Her mother's tale

London seems to be teeming with elderly people who immigrated to England from Central and Eastern Europe before WWII in the late thirties of the last century. When you least expect it, you come across their descendents, the first generation who became British by birth.

* * *

For many years I've phoned my consultant's secretary, a young-looking forty year old, to arrange appointments with the 'great man', both of us completely unaware that her mother's background was very similar to mine.

I cannot recall when we decided to have a little chat in the hospital's foyer or, time permitting, a cup of tea together in the cafeteria to exchange pleasantries about her boss's professional expertise. I told her that he views his patients not just as someone who needs medical advice, but also spares the time to find out their personal circumstances, such as their family and facilities at home.

"As a matter of fact," I said, "I owe him a great debt of gratitude for enabling my late husband, also an in-patient at the time, to visit me after surgery in my room by pushing his wheelchair. I cannot name one other doctor who would have shown me such kindness. This motivated me to give him a copy of one of my books from which he still cites passages."

"What is your book about?"

"Oh, it's my autobiography. As a fifteen-year old refugee from Germany I arrived in England via France. There, officials refused to extend my visa to remain in Paris after eight months of residency which, in the end, turned out to be one of many lucky breaks since I left my parents."

"What a coincidence! My mother came with a *Kindertransport* from Bonn. After her arrival she was sent to a couple in a small Midland's town who maltreated the ten year old. When they were out, the child had to wait in front of the house. No key was given to her to get back in, even in the cold weather or when it was raining.

One day when a local vicar saw her shivering on the doorstep, he took pity on her. He brought her to the vicarage and collected her few belongings, all fitting into the small suitcase which her grief-stricken mother had packed. She was cosseted by his wife and children. Fridays and Saturdays he drove her to the synagogue: mindful that she should not forget her heritage. Finally, he found a Jewish family to take her in. They were delighted. Theirs was a traditional Jewish home, like the one she had left behind.

"What a wonderful tale, Janice."

"She died fifteen years ago but had enjoyed a fulfilled life," the daughter added.

A quarter of an hour before my appointment to consult one of her employer's colleagues, we got down to the business of fixing a date to see her boss. From that day onwards we always had a little chat either in the hospital's entrance or, if she was not too busy, over a cup of tea in the cafeteria.

Sadly, she passed away suddenly after a haemorrhage, leaving behind a twice-widowed husband, over ten years her senior, who had cherished her.

"Who am I?"

Introduction

"You are not a proper Jew," was an accusation flung at me by two Jewish men some twenty years ago.

The first was meted out by a former Polish resistance fighter in WWII during a gathering of Holocaust survivors at the London Jewish Cultural Centre. He reasoned, as I was not a practising Jew and descended from a middle-class Central European family, I had hardly suffered enough, not having been in a concentration camp. Nor had I the slightest insight into the psyche of working-class Eastern Jews who had lived in their ghettos for generations, some of them self-imposed, for safety's sake.

With hindsight I realize he had a chip on his shoulder, like a former colleague of mine in a Whitechapel school, East London. He blamed me for having been able to pursue my studies a mere five years after my arrival in this country, while his great-grandfather from Poland had to earn his living as a hawker, his grandfather as a haberdashery stall-holder and his father as a shopkeeper. It was the proudest moment of his parents' life, so he told me, when he, his firstborn, enrolled as a scholarship student in a teachers training college. His brother's lot was to help in the shop.

The second time in a more insulting manner I was considered, the correct Yiddish word eludes me, to be more worthless than a non-Jew. As far as my neighbour was concerned, a descendent of Polish Jews (his forefathers had immigrated to England before the last decade of the 19th century), I had rejected my true identity. However much I tried to convince him that I owed it to my parents and to most of my extended family, all victims of the Final Solution in Auschwitz, never to abandon the faith of my forefathers, he obstinately maintained his negative opinion of me.

These two conversations led me to ask myself who am I or, in other words, how do I perceive myself? I also started to question neighbours, relations, friends and anyone else with whom I came into contact.

"Do not delve into your lineage," I warned them, "just question yourself who you believe you are."

* * *

Milk of human kindness did not flow through the veins of my brilliant professor of literature, a xenophobic blue-stocking.

"We English greet each other when we meet on the stairs, rather than utter a brief hello," she shouted at me in her impeccable Oxbridge accent in 1945, because I had dared to rush down the stairs in front of her. The rebuke "We English..." hit me like a bombshell. It implied, "You are an outsider, not One of Us."

Her unkind words hurt me deeply. I, a teenage Jewish refugee from Germany, had been classified as a friendly alien at the outbreak of hostilities. In spite of the British citizenship awarded me in November 1947, a year after I left the unreal world of academia, she and other bigots would continue to regard me as a foreigner.

* * *

After humiliating and degrading experiences because I did

not belong to the Aryan race during my childhood and early teens, I had erroneously believed that I had left the pecking order of 'pure' German or 'pure' English behind me. But I discovered later on that undue importance is still apportioned to one's nationality and class, rather than one's human positive attributes. Therefore I started compiling an informal questionnaire over half a century ago. I was struck by the many unexpected responses I received over the years.

Responses:

Mala (single, now in her early seventies, a carer of live-in mentally disturbed clients, employed by the local council), "I am a carer of Sri Lankan origin, British and owner of a property."

Gerry (married, mid-seventies, with an air of self-satisfaction), "I am English of Eastern European descent."

Rachel (a rabbi, married). In a typical Jewish manner, before answering she started posing questions. Finally she replied, "Jewish, nothing else."

Peter (single, mid-sixties, semi-retired). After hesitation, "A human being, British of Celtic origin."

Sandra (single, in her mid-sixties). With self-assurance, "Bell-ringer, retired social worker, British. I am a spiritual person."

Noel (married, seventy). "Irish."

Pat (his wife, mid-sixties). "English."

During one of our Tuesday lunches for OAPs at the London Jewish Liberal Synagogue, hosted by younger members of the congregation, I asked everyone sitting at my table.
Joan (now deceased), Brenda and Ken. "Jewish, of course."
Florence, "Scottish."
Bob (refugee from Germany before WWII). "British."
Tim (served during WWII), "British."
George, my late husband (served in WWII but would have refused to be deployed in Palestine). "I am British."

Frau Nuki (an upper-middle-class Austrian Jewish refugee in her eighties, a guest in my mother-in-law's boarding house some 50 years ago), "I am Viennese." She, alone, declined to apply for British citizenship.

I remember her dainty presence clearly and can imagine that she must have stood out among all the other adorned ladies who attended the balls at the Court of Franz Joseph before WWI during the 'Golden Age of Viennese Jewry'. She regretted deeply that her son became a Catholic as Jews were officially, later 'unofficially', barred from entering certain professions in Austria, even before the *Anschluss* (Hitler's Annexation of Austria in 1938).

John (retired teacher). "I am a Mixture of English, Eastern European and Welsh."

Renata (mid-thirties, accident assessor in her own country, now a house-help). "Mother, European, Polish."

Roy (late seventies some ten years ago). "Welsh."

Mariusz (gardener, early thirties). "Polish."

Sahill (early twenties). "Muslim/British in equal measure, both have their ups and downs."

Eka (in her early thirties). "Japanese."
Her mother (in her mid-sixties). "Japanese."

Paul (mini-cab driver, late fifties). "Catholic, Jesuit–educated turned Jewish."

Ann (Evelyn's daughter, married to an Australian, late fifties, Welsh, worshipping in a chapel). "I see myself as a Christian believer."

Evelyn (turned ninety years of age, born in Lancashire, Roy's wife, still living in North Wales). "I'm a widow, being officially cared for by Ann, my daughter."

Gita (early fifties, a carer in this country). "Teacher, Indian."

My answer to "Who am I?" a retired teacher, British, European, Jewish.

Conclusion:
Strangely enough, the respondents defined themselves by their nationality rather than their faith, with the exception of the rabbi and a few members of the congregation. Even the young Muslim who some five years ago refused to shake my Jewish hand, now feels allegiance to both 'in equal measure'.
 The fact that Gita's gut-reaction to "Who am I?" mirrored

mine, proved to me that the calling of a teacher is of overriding significance when answering this leading question.

"What is in my genes", I asked myself and looked once again at my maternal family tree.
The first entry refers to Joseph Trevis, Rabbi of Marseilles in 1343.
His son, Matthieu, was appointed *Grand Rabbin de Paris* by Charles V in 1363.
His descendents officiated as rabbis in Padua, Prague, Venice and other places of learning and enriched Jewish literature with seminal works. By the end of the 19th century, they shed rabbinical robes and became physicians or accountants. They settled in Berlin and Breslau. After Hitler came to power most of their descendents perished in the Holocaust, except those who had migrated to the United States or England, including myself.

In an ideal world labels, such as English, Muslim, German and others, would have lost their meaning and the universal answer to "Who am I?" should contain just three simple words, "A human being." This was my seventeen-year-old grandson's reply.

Unsolicited confessions

On that particular morning in August many tourists preferred to desert the sun-drenched valley. A gentle breeze was tracing tiny ripples on the blue, transparent lake. Everyone was eager to escape the rapidly increasing heat. They were gathered at the foot of the mountain on a narrow platform, hewn out of a grey, uneven rock face. Holidaymakers, dressed in thin colourful garments and open sandals, contrasted absurdly with Alpinists in full climbing gear. Other well-shod passengers would challenge their prowess on the less demanding *Wanderwege* (mountain paths). Railway enthusiasts, thrilled to be hauled up the mountain by a beautifully polished steam locomotive, made up the growing number.

As soon as one crowded train started the hour-long journey up the slope, the next was shunted into its place. The three of us clambered on board. Some passengers pushed themselves unceremoniously into the separate sections of the carriages to find a space on the wooden benches. Each accommodated eight persons, even well-endowed Swiss matrons. The doors were safely secured by the guard and, after a shrill sound of a whistle, the train began to chug alongside the mountain face spewing out coils of steam into the unpolluted atmosphere.

Enchanted by Nature's beauty drifting past us, liberated from the harsh realities of daily existence, we were transported into lofty heights by the long, snake-like vehicle. Its shiny red underbelly picked up every light and shade.

The passengers had settled down, talking softly. Their voices were muffled by the rhythmic hissing of the steam and the steady chatter of the engine. Occasionally a fidgety child, bored by the serenity outside, made some undue noise. It was reprimanded by the accompanying adults.

I was completely oblivious to the strangers facing us. A gentle tap on my shoulder brought me down to earth. My ever solicitous husband peered at me anxiously.

"Are you all right, darling? This gentleman is talking to you."

"*Madame*, you and your younger sister are a charming pair."

I noticed a square-faced, stout man. His white golf cap sat jauntily on his big head. An unbuttoned yellow shirt, exposing a heavy silver chain on his hairy chest, clashed blindingly with bright orange trousers.

Beady, roving eyes leered at us both, my daughter and me. It was the kind of lecherous look which makes a woman feel undressed. The phoney compliment, the sight of his ugly, fat hands ready to grope any female flesh within his reach, made me wince.

"You are too generous, sir. My so-called sister happens to be our daughter."

The train crept through a tunnel. Darkness and trapped steam invaded the open carriages. The woman by his side felt visibly uncomfortable.

"*Der Dampf tut mir nicht gut!*" ("I am feeling unwell in this air full of steam"), she exclaimed involuntarily.

The fibreglass adjustable windows had not been pulled down; soon we emerged into brilliant daylight; the pure Alpine air cleansed our lungs.

"*Sie sprechen deutsch.*" ("You speak German.") The cultured voice of the man's female companion was directed at me.

"My wife." Turning to his left, the colourful cavalier squeezed the thin arm of the woman at his side. "I mean, Anna, my playmate, the adopted wife," he corrected himself without explaining why he had 'adopted' her.

"*Sie spechen deutsch,*" the frail lady in a sober dress insisted.

"*Ja...*"

Her husband cut me short with an unwelcome tirade.

"I speak French. We have a house in the south of France. I, Solly Lipschitz," he stood up and saluted, "fought in the Resistance. But we also live in Los Angeles, near all the famous stars. Bespoke tailoring, that was my trade a long time ago."

He ran out of breath.

"You come to my house and open the cupboards; twenty handmade suits! And now I have earned the right to enjoy myself: travelling here, there and everywhere."

Within less than ten minutes, he had entertained us with the story of his life.

"Look at me! I am nearly seventy, fit and strong. My physical urges are still those of a young man," he added for good measure.

Nobody showed the slightest interest in this ridiculous revelation, least of all the Dutch honeymoon couple in the other corner of the compartment, completely absorbed in each other.

"*Tu ennuies tout le monde,*" ("You are boring everybody,") his wife whispered.

"*Quand je veux parler, je parle,*" ("When I want to say something, I do
so,") he replied enraged. His thick Eastern European accent assassinated the music of the elegant language with every

sound he uttered.

The fading light in the next tunnel ended the couple's squabble. Fierce eye-contact, which had punctuated their forcefully delivered words, had been lost.

"How could it be that the garish *parvenu* and the modest, cultivated lady could share the autumn of their lives together?" I wondered.

When daylight was once again restored, the young couple let go of their embrace. Anna had moved to the edge of the bench, as far away from her irate spouse as she could. She leaned across towards me.

In an urgent voice, in German, she told me that she had been born in Vienna. Her family had fled from the totalitarian *régime* in Russia. Life for members of the middle class (so-called 'exploiters of the honest worker') had become unsafe. After the annexation of Austria by the German Government, fearing the worst once again, her parents sent her to a finishing school in Switzerland.

"Will you speak English, for heaven's sake. I want to hear what fairy tales you are fabricating again."

His vicious look made her flinch. Lifting her eyes demurely towards him, she begged him to allow her to speak German. "I have so little opportunity to practice the language."

"First I was a pupil there; then I stayed on as a teacher. It was heaven on earth."

Anna's eyes shone as she recalled that period of her youth. It did not last. The colour of her face began to change; tears glistened in her eyes.

"My parents, my family, perished in the Holocaust."

Her last words were almost inaudible. The unfeeling brute, her husband, barged in.

"Now we have really heard more than enough. I want you to forget all that, everything German. I will not tolerate German in my house any more."

"But I will never forget the country's literature, the unequalled wealth of artistic achievement."

Her tired eyes began to search mine, imploring me to support her. I refused to take sides in the argument.

Abruptly, her husband changed the subject.

"Have you been to New Zealand?"

A rhetorical question; he continued without a pause.

"You ought to go there. A fine country! I prefer to live in the States. America is THE BEST," he emphasized, looking around the compartment for general approval of his statement.

Neither the Dutch couple (still in deep communion with each other), nor Anna, mortified by his boastful remarks, gave him that satisfaction. As for us, we tried to conceal our disgust. His trivial talk and the heartlessness, assumed or otherwise, towards his wife seemed quite perverse. Instinctively, I reached out my hands again and clasped hers in mine, as if to protect her.

"The tragic loss of my family, the trauma of the camp in which life was terminated by official decree, drove me to Palestine to fight for a Jewish State."

Her voice faltered; without avail, she searched for words to adequately convey the depth of her feelings. Then, she shrugged her shoulders hopelessly. With a sudden surge of willpower this pathetic, small human being pulled herself together.

"Somehow, a year later my boyfriend and I ended up in the States, in New York. I was pregnant. We wanted to get married. Joseph had a heart attack; he worried too much and could not cope with all the difficult immigration regulations. Nathan was born. I was a single mother."

Exhausted, she sank back into her seat.

"Yea. They didn't get hitched. He dropped dead. Out of the goodness of my heart I made an honest woman out of her. I adopted her bastard and gave them a roof over their heads. End of story!"

"It wasn't quite like that. We did want to get married," she protested.

She had not enlarged on how or where she lived before she met Solly. It occurred to me that she may have been supported by a Jewish organization. One of their agents might also have acted as matchmaker. Who could blame Anna for putting her baby's needs first, even if the prospective bridegroom's persona was far below her code of behaviour.

"Nathan is a do-gooder in Washington. He looks after drug-users,coloured kids, loafers," Solly jeered, implying clearly that he could not be the progenitor of someone who had never been able to find a 'proper' job.

Our daughter had watched the couple's interaction with amazement.

"It was just like a scene of marital strife on the stage," she said later.

The manicure case

Before I left home in mid-August 1938 to join distant relations in France, my family and I visited all the friends they had made since setting up home in Frankfurt shortly after the Great War.

The prospect of living in Paris, a town so vividly and enthusiastically described to us young teenagers by our French teacher in school, made me blissfully unaware of the perilous situation German Jews faced in Hitler's Third Reich and of the sad fact that I might never see my family again.

Years ago my parents had befriended an unusual couple. The bibliophile husband may have initially been one of my father's customers who sought his erudite advice when selecting one of the books, neatly stacked according to subject-matter, from the shelves of his University Bookshop which was frequented by lecturers and students of the nearby Johann Wolfgang Goethe University at the *Bockenheimer Warte*.

The couple occupied the maisonette of a modern apartment block in one of the town's fashionable districts. The four of us climbed up three or four flights of stairs, my mother and older brother, as usual, more slowly behind my father and me.

After reaching the top, he pushed the bell. A blue-eyed, Rubenesque woman, her corn-blond plaited hair trained round the crown of her head, opened the door.

She beamed down at me.

"So this is the little wanderer going off to live in Paris. You are a lucky girl."

She ushered us into a sunny room. Through the glass ceiling I saw the chestnut trees, their leaves fluttering in the breeze. Potted plants lined the windowsill. A vase filled with yellow roses stood on the hand-embroidered table-cloth.

The middle-aged, sickly looking man, dressed in a house-coat over a silk-shirt and tie, wheeled himself towards us.

"Paul, meet our friends' children. Isn't exciting! Helga is off to Paris in a few days. You'll miss your little sister, Kurt, won't you?"

He stretched out his pale hands; it disconcerted me to spot the blue veins under his yellowish skin. Before we left our flat, and during our walk there on foot, my parents had told us that *Onkel* Paul was unable to walk. *Tante* Maria was helping him to be as comfortable as possible and only went out to go to the local shops. We were instructed not to stare at the invalid, so different from all the other adults we had come into contact with and to very politely address them as *Onkel* Paul and *Tante* Maria.

"But they are not our REAL relations," my brother, a stickler for truth, interposed.

"Never mind that. And be sure to say thank you when you are given something and don't forget the important little word 'please'," my mother reminded us.

"They are not used to children," my father added. "So do not speak, unless you are spoken to."

"Why don't they have children? All your other friends have children," Kurt wanted to know.

"Being so sick *Onkel* Paul could not have been the kind of father who can take his family on hikes in the Taunus or see the pretty towns along the Rhine from the steamers, and *Tante* Maria has to look after him day and night."

Paul was a highly intelligent man who had travelled abroad before he had lost the use of his legs; none of his faculties had been impaired. It was fascinating to hear him talk about Paris, the years he had studied at the Sorbonne and all the historical places he had seen. That day, I promised myself I would follow in his footsteps when I was a grown-up.

My brother Kurt who had been adept in taking his toy cars to pieces in his childhood, dismantling and putting his bicycle together again in his teens, stared at the vehicle in which our newly-found uncle was sitting. No doubt he wondered how the different components worked, until he was more attracted by the sight and smell of the home-baked pastries *Tante* Maria brought from the kitchen. My parents had warned us "not to make pigs of ourselves" (not their exact words), he did just that.

I had noticed the little parcel on the sideboard, neatly wrapped in coloured paper and tied with a red ribbon. It occurred to me that this might be a present for me; I had never gone away empty- empty from my family's acquaintances.

With an effort of will, *Onkel* Paul wheeled himself across the room on the spotlessly clean parquet floor and picked it up.

"Helga, this is a gift from us to you. You may open it now if you like."

Very carefully I undid the wrapping, mindful of my mother's counsel, "never waste anything which might come in handy later," and caught a first glimpse at the oblong, red leather case. I unfastened the silver button. On the bed of brown suede lining I discovered a pair of scissors and a seven-piece manicure grooming-kit with mother of

pearl handles necessary to shape, sculpt and polish nails.
"What a wonderful present. I have never had anything like that," I called out. I ran to *Tante* Maria who sat near her husband and gave her a big hug. Then I gingerly grasped one of *Onkel*'s fragile hands, fearing I might break his fingers in my excitement.

Tears trickled down *Tante* Maria's cheeks when I thanked her again and again. Many years later, as I manicured my nails with these little tools, I remembered the expression on her face and wondered if my great joy that day had intensified her sorrow at having been denied motherhood.

During our walk back to our modest attic flat (after the boycott of Jewish shops we exchanged it in the spring of 1933 for the six-room apartment in which Kurt and I had grown up), I heard him whine, "Helga always gets all the attention and presents."

Both my parents were worried about my imminent departure into the 'wide world' so they paid no attention to him.

I have never found out what became of the couple. After the war I learned that the Nazis made short shrift of handicapped people, considered to be 'a burden to the State', by euthanasia or mass execution. *Onkel*'s situation was made worse by his Jewish faith.

His wife, Maria, with a pure Aryan, Germanic pedigree, would have had to choose between annulling the marriage or suffer the same fate meted out to the Jews. But she had been a nurse, devoted to her patients, among them Paul. He had appreciated fully the care Nurse Maria took of him in hospital and sensed that she had even become fond of him.

Before his discharge, the paraplegic plucked up enough courage to ask her if she would become his wife. That was about eight years ago; she was in her mid-thirties and he ten years her senior.

Remembering the deep affection with which she treated her ailing husband, as well as her unswerving commitment, I am almost certain that she did not desert Paul and stayed loyal to him until the bitter end. That is why I have kept the red leather case in one of my bedroom drawers until this day, even though the suede lining is torn in places and the little tools are no longer safe to use.

The Infant prodigy

Kristina, partially anglicized to Christina when her mother was separated and then divorced, returned to her Swedish father but came back later to London. She became what was then called 'bosom friends' with my daughter, both pupils at a Hampstead public school for girls. The statuesque, blond, blue-eyed girl visited us very frequently and liked to sit in our roomy kitchen with Fluffy, our white cat, on her lap.

"Why is she so fond of Fluffy and never picks up Beauty?" our daughter asked, once her friend had left.

"She seems to identify with her for no obvious reason. But my experience as a teacher has shown me that a child's distress at having only one parent is somewhat assuaged by cradling a pet. When she sees us being together as a happy family it must intensify her longing for fatherly love. Just being with him during holidays or during his short business visits to London cannot compensate for his daily absence."

Both girls went to university after 'A' levels; Christina, exceptionally gifted, to Cambridge, our daughter to Bristol. They did not lose touch, met during vacations and occasionally she, mature for her age and even more beautiful than before, came to our house. When Fluffy had to be put down due to breathing problems in her old age, she grieved for the little feline she had loved so much.

* * *

Christina was the first to get married. Edward, she always called him Eddie, had been one of her fellow-students. The quiet, small, short-sighted intellectual, his brown-rimmed glasses obscuring part of his pale face, was introduced to us soon afterwards. Before going home she wrapped a woollen scarf round his neck on that cold winter afternoon, handed him his fur cap and bent down to button up his coat. He did not resist being treated like a helpless specimen.

I realized that the maternal affection she had felt for the cat had been transferred to him. He seemed to be comfortable with and relished her devoted attention. Eddie's parents, dedicated to their careers, had left him to grow up under the supervision of a nanny. (This I learnt later.)

Christina, already ambitious as a school girl, strove resolutely to improve her position as a lecturer; she became one of the youngest principals of a London university college. Her husband, in a less spectacular manner, advanced as the head of research in a pharmaceutical enterprise. Financially sound, they decided that the time was ripe to have a child. All had been carefully planned beforehand. Her mother, a wealthy widow and lady of leisure, would come to live in a fully furnished luxury apartment nearby and care for the baby with the help of Christina's former English nanny after the end of her daughter's maternity leave.

* * *

Shortly before his third birthday Simon was enrolled in the nursery class of the local state junior school. His parents wanted him to rub shoulders with children from less advantageous environments, although both had benefitted from attending prestigious public schools in London. They belonged to the large group of 'armchair' socialists who nevertheless maintained a life-style completely at odds with their blue-collar 'brethren'. Eddie, more sensitive than his wife, was honest enough to admit that their advantaged background was in complete contrast to the ideal of living in an 'equal society'.

Simon had certainly inherited his parents' thirst for knowledge. By the time he was two years old he remembered nursery rhymes read to him. A year later he could read them himself. His favourite was 'Simple Simon met a pieman, Going to the fair...' which he recited, all sixteen lines, as his party piece the Sunday afternoon the family came to us for tea.

Graciously he accepted our applause with a bow. As an 'encore' he sang, as rhythmically as he had done the rhyme, "I like it, I like it. It's about Simon. I am not", emphasizing 'not', "simple. I am not simple."

Then, imitating a grown-up voice which sounded like squeaks, he said, "It was first published in 1764, mummy told me so and daddy is just teaching me how to play chess."

He looked at us to see if his announcements had impressed us. We did not move a muscle. In revenge, he pointed to a corner of the ceiling and chirped again rhythmically,

"There are cobwebs, there are cobwebs."

His parents thought that this was funny and laughed.

A few weeks after the infant prodigy's performance we came across them in the cafeteria of the National Gallery. Eddie manoeuvred the pushchair at the counter behind Simon who held on to his mother's hand.

"Mummy," he shouted at the top of his voice, "there are

your friends, the ones with the cobwebs."

The people in the queue followed his gaze and smiled.

None of the tables were free, so they decided to sit with us, Simon in a high chair, Eddie on a chair he had moved away from a couple's table.

"Isn't he a bit too young to visit art galleries?" I queried, watching the infant devouring a cream cake, crumbs sticking round his mouth.

"Certainly not!" Christina exclaimed. "Simon is particularly interested in Italian Renaissance paintings. He is already so excited that we intend to visit the galleries in Rome and Venice."

The former school friends caught up with the news of the other 'old girls' in their year, until Simon jabbed an outstretched finger into his mother's side.

"I'm bored," he piped. "Daddy, can I read 'The Times' while the women are nattering about their school days."

Straight away Christina turned her attention to him, lifted him on her lap and spread out the newspaper in front of him. When he was sure everyone was listening, he began to read aloud a paragraph from the front page. His parents were ecstatic; to them it sounded as if he had understood the passage.

We have not seen them again since that chance meeting at the gallery.

* * *

In the meantime we have been blessed with a highly intelligent grandson, a budding thespian. To our great relief his parents let their child develop according to his age, enjoy the company of his contemporaries, rather than force-feed him with information, and wait until he is ready to explore the world around us by himself. I wonder what has become of the infant prodigy. Has he freaked out, freed from his parents' tight leach; or is he now, probably in his mid-thirties, a confirmed bachelor, completely immersed in his profession to the exclusion of everything else?

The Psychotherapists

1

During and after my teaching career, I had to deal with three psychotherapists. The first, a distinguished looking, corpulent professor in his mid-forties, treating patients in his Harley Street consulting room, had exchanged his dowdy wife for his attractive, blond receptionist. To be close to little Sylvie, his daughter, he chose to live in the same street as his family. The mother, too weak to fight for her rights after having been deserted, allowed him free access.

Sylvie had befriended our daughter in the private nursery where they played and sat together. Their teacher was kind enough to feed and look after the child until a parent was free to pick her up. On Fridays, the day I worked full-time, my daughter was also left in Mrs Bolton's care.

She used to busy herself with household chores after lunch while the children played with the many toys she had ready for them in another room. Every so often she would peep at them through the door, especially when they were suddenly very quiet.

One afternoon, checking up on them, as usual, she saw them both with their frilly knickers down to their ankles, standing face-to-face, exploring each other below the waist.

"I withdrew," she told me over a cup of tea, "and just called them, as usual, for a beaker of milk and their favourite cake."

"Did my daughter talk about the new, strange game they

had played?"

"No. She just looked at me somewhat bewildered and ran towards me as I came into the room. I asked them to pull their knickers up. I am really sorry about their strange behaviour, definitely initiated by Sylvie, who is no more her former sunny self. She has become a highly disturbed child. Under these circumstances I would fully understand if you decided to make different arrangements."

I assured her that my trust in her ability to care for and teach nursery age children had not been diminished, but, due to little Sylvie's inappropriate behaviour, our house-help would collect my daughter at noon on Fridays, give her lunch and then bring her to my school for the afternoon session.

It turned out to be a success, as the older children in my class treated her like a princess, which she thoroughly relished.

2

During the last fifteen years of my career, I taught modern languages in a school for physically handicapped pupils. I recall the day when a highly intelligent boy who had lost the power of one of his limbs, due to an accident while playing cricket in his grammar school, joined my class. He found it hard to come to terms with his disability. After some weeks he managed to concentrate on his studies, like the other five fourteen to sixteen-year-old high achievers who eventually passed GCSE and 'A' level exams.

During our staff meetings we used to discuss the emotional state of a particular child with the psychotherapist, as highly charged pupils often used to calm down during or after treatment.

Dr. Maureen Hall (she wore her own emotions on her sleeve), often chatted with me about our offspring. She had brought up two sons. The eldest was happily married to a girl he had met at university; the youngest had committed suicide.

"Sam had always been an introvert. He had no real friends and refused to go to parties or the theatre with his brother whose wife-to-be tried to introduce him to eligible young women. We hoped one of them might be a suitable partner for him.

"Perhaps he felt that his sibling had always stolen all the limelight: being exceptionally gifted academically and a much sought-after cricket player by county clubs. Perhaps we had been too exhilarated about John's forthcoming marriage and did not involve Sam enough. Unwittingly, I should have known better, we left him to his own morbid devices.

"During his student days he seemed to be stressed whenever he came back at weekends. I will always blame myself for not detecting he suffered from depression; he would never talk about himself, even to his brother. My husband and I were confident that in the stable environment of our home he would become more relaxed after his Finals and his sombre moods would gradually evaporate. It was not to be. I failed him and he took his own life."

She gave no indication as to where and when.

* * *

After leaving school Maureen decided to study psychotherapy. "For no particular reason, except that most of the other girls chose subjects which would lead to a

teaching career, and I thought I was not cut out for it."
   The core course lasted three years. As a twenty-two year old who had never been away from home, she did not feel mature enough to choose a field of psychotherapy to specialize in. Children and adolescents, adults or people with drug problems; each area entailed another three years before qualifying.

For almost a year she was at a loose end trying to find her inner self by taking stock of her potential. Being the eldest, she had always loved looking after her three younger siblings and organised their parties when on occasions a dozen or so friends came to her home. It seemed quite natural to her that her career should be closely linked to children. As soon as someone had suggested to her she should consider educational psychotherapy, it struck her that treating a youngster's mind was just as important as treating his body. As soon as she had qualified and had been appointed to visit special schools, she acknowledged she had found her destiny.

During my training I had attended lectures in psychology, therefore I was extremely interested in her work. Away from the other staff, we spent lunch-time breaks together in my classroom whenever she was free to do so.
   "Everything seemed to be so straight forward. I had married the young man who had patiently courted me until I was settled in my career. I brought up two sons and went back to work when the youngest had started school. My mother was ever ready to help out when I would be delayed at work. Then out of the blue all our lives were shattered by Sam's wilful deed," Maureen admitted. "Yet I had to be strong for my husband's and the young couple's sake. I

searched for an answer as to why I had failed my younger son in the psychology text books I kept but had never opened since my student days. My husband told me to concentrate on something which would absorb me. That was the moment I made up my mind to contact the Samaritans and offer my services."

Now she spends a few hours at weekends listening to troubled children and adolescents who have no one else to turn to.

"Their parents are unaware, of their offspring's emotional turmoil, just like we were. It's such a pity that this service is anonymous, as parents cannot be warned of what might be in store for them," she said, as great sadness crept into her face.

3

As a ten-year-old pupil in my second year in the liberal Jewish Grammar school in Frankfurt (orthodox parents enrolled their children in the other Jewish school in the East End), I came face to face with a *Mischling*, a mongrel. This insulting term was given by the Nazis to children whose genes were 'mixed' (the verb *mischen* means 'to mix') with 50 percent of non-Aryan, pure German blood. My friends and I could only guess which one of her parents were Jewish. Our teachers did not disclose any personal details about our new classmate who was a head taller than us, nor were we interested enough in her to ask. Indeed, not one of us cared to befriend her.

It was the practice in German schools that non-achieving children had to remain in the same year if they failed to get results which would allow them to move up after Easter (the school year began after the holidays) with the rest of his or her class. This was most aptly called *sitzen bleiben*, to remain sitting.

When I myself experienced what it meant to be the 'odd one out' in a Church of England teachers' training college, I belatedly sympathised with the *Mischling* who was sidelined, even looked at with suspicion, because she was not one hundred percent Jewish.

* * *

In the late 1970s I became acquainted with another *Mischling* here in London. Her father was Jewish and had thought it wise to send his daughter and her older brother to a boarding school in England before the outbreak of WWII, although their parents did not practice any religion, nor had they ever enlightened them about their Jewish heritage.

Young Martha, unable to speak or understand English, was completely alienated in her new surroundings until, after intensive tuition by one of the teachers, she was sufficiently fluent to converse with the other boarders. In conversation, she told them why she had been sent abroad rather than going to a school in the town where she was born.

After half-term, one of the girls, the daughter of narrow-minded, anti-Semitic, Christian zealots started to cold-shoulder her and spread rumours about the Jews. She made hurtful remarks about her and reminded all the fellow-boarders that the Jews were responsible for the crucifixion of Jesus Christ. It became unbearable for her, especially as the members of staff were at a loss as how to handle the mischievous girl. It would have been against the school's interest to send her down. They feared repercussions as her father was a very influential person. To their great relief Martha stuck it out and promised to herself that she would embrace the Jewish faith as soon as she left the hated school.

* * *

Both her parents survived the war; her mother in Germany, her father, after hiding in various countries in Europe (before they were occupied by the German Army), finally ended up in Shanghai.

Martha's brother returned to Germany and married a German girl. She was reunited with her father in this country. They set up home and the fifteen year old finished her education in a public day school nearby.

They became members of a liberal synagogue. After an intensive religious education, she was confirmed. (Orthodox Jews do not tolerate Bat-Mitzwah.) Only on very rare and special occasions did she return to Germany to see her mother and brother, remaining on friendly terms.

* * *

Martha trained as a teacher. During one of the synagogue's social events she was introduced to a young man, a psychiatrist by profession. He fully understood that the separation from her home at an early age had left an indelible scar and realized that concentrating on her work had a beneficial therapeutic effect on her. She was appointed deputy head in her early thirties shortly after the maternity leave of her second child.

As the offspring grew up she wondered what effect the story of her past would have on them. She and her husband felt adamant that nothing should be concealed from the second generation. They had waited to talk to them until they were old enough to appreciate the individual fate of their mother in the wider context of Holocaust history. As a result, they were able to cope with it. However, Martha soon discovered that many children of Holocaust survivors were unable to deal with their parents' traumatic experiences and needed counselling. She also realised that others–there were many among the congregation–developed mental amnesia, the memory being too painful to be conjured up into their consciousness.

With her husband's approval she left the teaching profession and embarked on a course of psychotherapy, which would also help to alleviate her still persistent mental stress.

She qualified. Her patients are some of the children of 'the second generation' who flock to professionals like Martha in the hope of gaining sufficient strength to enjoy a normal life instead of agonising over their parents' past.

Felix

In my mind's eye I still see the shadowy figure, slumped in an upholstered chair near a corner of the window in the kitchen in my mother-in-law's boarding house for elderly refugees from Nazi oppression before WWII. Her own mother had sat in it until she passed away. I remember that Alice, too, used to flop into it after dinner had been served to the guests.

This was at the beginning of 1951. Felix died a week or so later, shortly after his sixty-ninth birthday.

"You would have got on famously with him, exchanging ideas and experiences," his son, my husband, told me when he put the last framed photo of his parents on the chest of drawers opposite the bed in our new home.

He and his mother had always spoken with great love and tenderness they had felt for him. Relying on their detailed descriptions, I could piece together the story of his childhood and youth. But I wanted to know much more about his later life and carefully scrutinised the few official documents marked, 'WOLFF papers', which my husband had put into our filing cabinet. There was a birth certificate, issued in Hackney, London, on the 21st December 1882; a new British passport, issued on the 10th of September 1937 and a death certificate, issued in Hampstead on the 15th January 1951. A German document, dated 31st October 1908, certified the registration of his marriage to *Fräulein* Alice Brody in Berlin-Charlottenburg.

His life curves like an arc from humble beginnings in London's East End to the pinnacle of his professional career in Berlin in the 1920s, and his decline a decade later back in London, deprived of active fulfilling years.

Gifted with a brilliant mind, he must have had an easy passage from an East End junior school to final examinations in a grammar school, excelling in English language and literature, as well as German, the native tongue of his mother, Ada.

After leaving school he applied for and obtained a position as a trainee reporter at the Daily Chronicle, amalgamated with other broadsheets in the 1960s. The reports he filed were of such a high standard that he was promoted to be a foreign correspondent in Berlin shortly after the turn of the century. With his mother's letter of introduction to her former school friend, Agnes Benscher, married to Abraham Brody, Felix gained entry into his family's large apartment in one of the up-market districts in the German capital.

Abraham, a successful entrepreneur, tall and still handsome, sized up the short, stocky young man, not born into the middle-class, with distaste. As soon as it was polite to do so, he retreated into his study, dismissing Felix as a non-entity with a small income, not worthy of his attention.

Alice, his eldest, was fascinated by this stranger from England, his amusing anecdotes and charming manner. Like a breath of fresh air, he dispelled the serious, constricting atmosphere imposed by the stern paterfamilias who ruled the household with a rod of iron.

In spite of his visible coldness towards Felix, Abraham could not refuse him admittance to his home because, for once, his wife Alice and her two younger siblings, a brother and a sister, lined up against him. Ungraciously, he tolerated the young man's presence. Whenever Felix was not working he found a pretext to visit the family, always seeking Alice's company.

Ada was a romantic, betrothed to an unsentimental bridegroom chosen by her father, according to the mores of the time. Within a few weeks their friendship had blossomed into love and it was she who encouraged the twenty-six-year-old suitor to ask Abraham for their daughter's hand in marriage. Alice was two years younger than him.

Abraham stalled, wanting to cool the young man's ardour.

"It is my duty to insist that any future husband of one of my daughters should be in a position to support his wife equal to the high standard to which she is accustomed. When you have the means to do so, you may ask me again."

Spurred on by his future father-in-law's caveat, Felix explored other sources of income. He penned advertising slogans for household and other products which were published in the press and broadcast on the radio in the *Rundfunk* (the nationwide broadcasting corporation). One of them I remember from my childhood; '*Schreibste ihm, schreibste ihr, schreibste auf MK-Papier*'. ('If you write to him, if you write to her, write on MK writing paper'), manufactured during that period in Max Krause's factory in Frankfurt-on-Main.

The profits from this new line of business enabled him to earn more than enough to rent an apartment near the Brodys (not quite as big as theirs), employ a maid and pay for luxury items, including presents for Alice's mother and sister. Both were delighted and, as far as they were concerned, Felix's arrival in their home was a relief from the daily mundane routine.

"After all, though this is not exactly an arranged marriage, Felix has been conventionally introduced to us," she remarked to her unenthusiastic spouse on the eve of the wedding. "Alice did not elope like a friend's daughter with her beau because of her intransigent father."

"Tittle-tattle. Other people's problems are of no concern to me whatsoever Ada. I promise you that I will not be swayed again when it is Betty's turn. That young man will be thoroughly vetted by me, as well as the girl our son chooses to be his wife."

Extremely reluctantly he gave his daughter away to the young journalist in one of Berlin's liberal synagogues, still upset that Felix was born on the wrong side of the tracks. On the wedding day he barely managed to smile or to partake of the six-course meal in the far end of the sumptuous ballroom in one of the capital's luxury hotels. Surveying the bridal couple and their friends on the dance floor, he nevertheless felt satisfied that he had impressed the many business contacts he had invited. The small fortune he had spent had not been in vain.

Abraham came to rue his words regarding the other two offspring. His son, Henri, 'married out'; thus committing the gravest sin. His daughter, Betty, became the wife of a bombastic ne'er-do-well, recently returned from New York where he was supposed to have made a fortune.

To prove it, he had beguiled mother and daughter with expensive gifts, all bought on credit. The marriage ended in divorce a year later after the birth of a son. His father-in-law refused to pay the creditors who knocked at the young couple's door. To the relief of the whole family, he vanished and was never heard of or seen again.

* * *

Alice and Felix considered themselves to be the happiest couple on earth. The young wife, liberated from her former surroundings, was able to read modern and classic literature without constantly being interrupted by her demanding mother and siblings, which she discussed with her erudite husband after they had eaten the *gourmet* meals she had copied from newly bought cookery books.

Often, in the afternoon, her mother visited her with her sister, now treating her married daughter as an equal. They appreciated the easy-going atmosphere in the young couple's home and chatted about their friends and neighbours. The maid, in a black dress with a white collar and apron, served coffee and cakes she had baked under Alice's supervision in the morning.

Felix, although a book-lined study awaited him, preferred to write at a table in the corner of his *Stammlokal* (favourite restaurant), frequented by his colleagues and people from the entertainment world, drinking many cups of black coffee. Even politicians used to come and relax from their arduous task of piloting the Ship of State in what they believed was the right direction (not always approved of by Kaiser William II during and pre-WWI), and afterwards by the new German democratic government of the Weimar Republic.

Thus Felix's circle of acquaintances widened, everyone being impressed by his extensive knowledge of cultural topics and political affairs. From time to time he used to arrive home with a cohort of friends near midnight when Alice had to dress up in her finest and wake up the maid. Between them they prepared late suppers for the men, engrossed in conversations about the events of the day and the imminent danger of war.

During WWI many British and other foreign nationals residing in Germany were rounded up and brought to *Ruheleben*, an internment camp near Berlin. Due to the fact that both his mother and wife, naturalised by marriage, were German by birth he was not detained. He may have had protection from someone in the echelons of power. It was mentioned that he was able to pass on information, using a pseudonym, about the home front in Berlin, via secret channels to Switzerland. Possibly he might have been engaged in missions unbeknown even to his wife. (No record ever existed.)

The only dark cloud on the otherwise blue horizon was the fact that even after ten years of marriage no child had been conceived, so much desired by the couple and Alice's doting mother. However, while there were no certainties during the hostilities, they decided to wait until the end of the war when normality had been restored.

* * *

After the Armistice in 1918 Felix's professional career found wings. All his previous social and political networking paid off. In spite of inflation of forty-one percent per day by October 1923, caused by the collapse of the political system during the war and the Weimar Republic's shaky economy, cultural life in Berlin had risen like a phoenix from the ashes which offered Felix an entry into the theatrical scene. He had written critiques of plays for the German press before, apart from sending overviews of the speedy, cultural recovery to his English editors. Yet he reached the zenith of his career when he was offered the post of co-producer at Berlin's *Komische Oper*, a venue for political satire and provocative dancing (a criminal offence during the Kaiser's reign), though not quite as blatant as at the *Moulin Rouge* in Paris.

Berlin had become a haven for transvestites, homosexuals, deviants of society and others living in the fast lane. In cabarets the younger generation of the middle classes whose parents who had wisely moved their assets abroad before the war or had benefitted from the brief economic revival after the inflation, as well as working class girls employed in shops, offices and banks gathered, 'to let their hair down' in an abandonment never known before, to the disgust of their elders.

Not only behaviour patterns changed radically, but also fashion. The new 'mode' dictated the *Bubikopf* (Eton-cut), a bobbed, short haircut with cloche hats, drop-waist dresses, furs and beaded necklaces down to the chest.

In England (not to be outdone by their Continental peers), the Flappers in the Roaring Twenties considered themselves to be 'the new women'. They espoused the spirit of the time, danced the Charleston, imported from New York, in jazz clubs and went to vaudeville shows.

Felix, always on call in his new role in the theatre, spent little time at home. Alice, still childless, suffered from his neglect of her needs. In sheer desperation she sought medical help. After undergoing various treatments their son was born in 1921.

She was jubilant. Surely now, she thought, her husband would rather be at her side rather than spend practically all his waking hours in the theatre. In vain, he tried to convince her that his schedule was as hectic as before, however much he wanted to be at home.

Felix's keen perception of the audience's preferences was such that he was chosen to select *'les girls'* who would appear on the stage in *tableaux vivants*: nudes in various settings who, according to censorship regulations, were forbidden to move. Two photographs handed down to us depict him with the troupe on tour. In one, all the blond beauties had just boarded the coach. In the other, they were lying naked on top of a vast bed in lascivious poses. He, with an air of satisfaction on his face, stands conspicuously in front of the scene.

His wife, accompanied by her sister, went to the premiere of the new show. Alice, herself, was extremely good-looking; so much so, that predatory males bestowed admiring glances on her. She took it in her stride, but the sight of the naked females in *'das lebende Bett'* shook her to the core. Grasping her younger sibling's hand she left during the interval.

Felix had wanted to show off both women. He was not amused. A bitter row broke out as soon as he returned home, even later than usual, after a boisterous party to revel in the audience's enthusiastic applause.

How was he to cope with his dual existence? In the real world he was supposed to be the attentive, loving husband and father; while in the make-believe world of the theatre alluring young women were enticing males to follow their sexual urges, thus undermining the fabric of society.

In rehearsal, every girl vied to be singled out as the lead dancer. It was up to Felix to choose the most attractive one after the choreographer had perfected a new routine. Naturally, the girls threw themselves at him. It never occurred to him that his power as the co-director to 'hire and fire', not his charisma , drew the competing girls to him.

A long-legged, platinum-blond Venus managed to secure the important part in the show. Her disappointed rivals busily spread the rumour that the girl was Felix's mistress. It reached Alice's ears.

Her first reaction was to discredit the vicious gossip. Yet in sheer desperation, she dyed her lustrous black hair blond, had it cut in the *Bubikopf* style and bought a dress of the latest fashion. What was becoming for a young, modern woman did not suit her. By then she was approaching her fortieth year.

Her plan to win back her errant husband misfired utterly.

"What on earth have you done to your hair and what is that fancy dress?" he exclaimed when she went to meet him at the door of their apartment.

"I thought you prefer blondes," she whimpered.

"Aha! And who has been telling tales?"

Felix considered himself to be the injured husband. He had just ended the affair and had promised himself to be faithful henceforth. He glared at her.

"I have come home early to spend some time with you and our baby before going on tour tomorrow. Obviously this is not to be."

Having packed another suit, two shirts, a change of underwear and toiletries in his portmanteau, he returned to the theatre and settled down for the night on the *chaise longue* in his office, leaving a distraught wife who ran back to her mother with the baby in arms.

There, she cried her eyes out, vowing she would never ever go back home. Ada, her wise mother, soothed her but refused to get involved in the marital strife. She wondered whether some of the blame should be apportioned to her daughter for she was not seen often enough in the theatre, wasting too much time as the ideal housewife, oblivious of the responsibilities of a co-director's wife.

* * *

Felix remained in Amsterdam with the giddy, excited, young women, eager to explore the notorious red light district in Holland's capital where prostitutes sat by their windows eyeing the potential male clientele.

Felix, ever anxious lest one of them would tear herself from their chaperone's tight leash during such excursions, followed them at a distance. At night, he patrolled the long corridors of the hotel to ensure that there were no prowlers about and that they were tucked up in bed, getting the sleep they needed to be in form for their strenuous dancing routines in the show.

By then in his mid-forties, responsible for the welfare of his troupe in addition to his duties as the producer, as well as dealing with his Dutch counterparts, he strained his energy to its limits. He began to long for the comforts of his home, so lovingly provided by his wife. He looked forward to a week's holiday after the end of the tour.

With a big bunch of red roses, full of anticipation, he quickly unlocked the front door. It was already past midnight; therefore he was not surprised everything was dark. He tiptoed into the bedroom ready to embrace his wife. The bed had not been slept in. He knocked at the maid's door. There was no reply. She had left too. In the tidy kitchen the ice box, usually containing enough food to feed over a dozen guests, stood empty.

Felix sat down in despair: Alice had always been there, done his bidding at any time of the day and night, been faithful and had never made any unreasonable demands. He suddenly realized how much he had taken her for granted lately, had rarely shown his gratitude or made her feel special. In short, he was more wedded to the theatre than to his wife and had failed as a husband.

Alice, being pampered by her mother as never before, had ample time to review her situation. She contemplated what the future might have in store for her and her baby. She weighed up her options; she feared she might end up as a divorcee, like her sister. After careful deliberation, she came to the conclusion that her love for Felix was everlasting. Given the chance, she would be prepared to weather the storm, were he to show the slightest sign of remorse.

After a restless night, Felix got up early. He was starving, not having had a morsel to eat since his return. He went to a nearby cafe and ordered breakfast. Bodily fortified, he was ready to 'face the music'. Would Alice merely bear a grudge, or would she be so deeply wounded that a reconciliation seemed unlikely?

Not knowing what to expect, he rushed up the flight of stairs, two at a time, to his parents-in-law's first floor apartment, resolved to win back his wife, even if he had to go down on bended knees. Life without her ubiquitous presence and the loss of his son would be unbearable.

The maid opened the door and ushered him into the lounge. Glancing round the walls, he noticed to his horror that some of the precious ornaments and original paintings had vanished. It occurred to him straight away that Abraham had sold anything of value to ride out the inflation in order to keep his family afloat.

Alice entered the room not uttering a word. It dawned on him that ageing had enhanced her beauty, as she directed her corn-flower eyes towards him. She waited for him to speak.

"There is no excuse for my behaviour. I sincerely regret I caused you so much pain, my darling, due to my absences and yes, my one and only affair. I cannot undo the past. But I can truthfully say that I have never stopped loving you and our child. So, however trite this might sound, I implore you to give me another chance to prove myself. I could not face life without you as my constant companion," he pleaded. "Please come back to our home."

This probably happened towards the end of the decade; their son must have been eight or nine years old. He was so used to staying with his *Oma* and *Opa* who, to his mother's dismay, always spoilt him, that he did not take what he called "my parents stupid quarrels" seriously, agreeing with the other boys in his class that grown-ups can be very, very silly.

* * *

The early Thirties ushered in the beginning of the end of the irresponsible, wanton nightly conduct of the younger generation. The Weimar Republic had crumbled in early spring of 1933 under the iron heel of the National Socialist Party. At its helm was Adolf Hitler, *der Führer*, a painter, recipient of the Iron Cross for bravery in the Great War. He had been rejected by the artistic establishment before the war and blamed the Jews.

Everything changed. Revues and all political parties

were banned. Some theatres were closed. Literature offending the National Socialist Party's ethos was burnt. Draconian measures were swiftly introduced, including the persecution of foreigners, Jews and homosexuals. No marriages were permitted between Aryans and Jews–lest this pure race would be contaminated by inferior blood.

Henceforth, Germanic traditions and values were to be followed. Anyone who contravened the new laws imposed on the '*Volk*' (the German population) was severely punished or deported to concentration camps.

Felix's work in the theatre came to an abrupt end. So did his contributions to the German press, strictly censored for any alien influence or departure from the Third Reich's principles. The income from his advertising slogans dried up.

Again and again he warned the English government and population of the growing danger posed by the armament drive in Germany, as well as drawing attention to Hitler's harangues during Nazi party rallies at *Nürenberg*. From the podium *der Führer* vociferated that Germany had been cheated of land and assets by the Versailles Treaty drawn up after WWI, as well as being betrayed by Jewish elements whose money had been removed abroad. His words were inflammatory: he claimed that members of the middle class had been deprived of their livelihood and that honest German workers had suffered most during the post-war years. He, alone, could be their saviour, he proclaimed.

They believed him and flocked to his party in their thousands. The unemployed were marshalled into building the *Autobahn* and other construction projects, apart from being recruited to make weapons in the armament factories.

The population was jubilant and worshipped Hitler as if he were a deity, hysterical women swooned at the sight of him. Felix's descriptions about Germany's new regime were published in the *Daily Chronicle*, as well as in other broadsheets. They were discussed on the radio during interviews with political commentators. However, the alarm bells fell on deaf ears in Downing Street.

As a result of the economic downturn, Abraham's finances were at their lowest ebb. The dispossession of his apartment made his family homeless. Generous as ever and never bearing a grudge, Felix, without hesitation, offered his in-laws a home in his spacious apartment and paid for all their expenses.

The Wolffs and the Brodys, lived together quite amicably. Alice's mother and sister adjusted well to the sudden change. Abraham, bereft of his wealth and autonomy, felt humiliated that his family had to be kept by his daughter's husband whom, in spite of all his generosity, the proud man still rated below his own status.

By the end of 1934, Nazi party members had infiltrated the press. Vigilantes spied on the professional and private lives of journalists. They joined the *habitués* during their nightly discussions in cafes, always listening, rather than talking. Anyone who criticised or disagreed with the government's policies was arrested at dawn the following morning and imprisoned; his fate hanging by a thread.

It must have been at the beginning of 1935 when a colleague of his, a member of the party for professional reasons only, warned Felix that he was being watched, followed wherever he went and that his British citizenship would not guarantee his safety. So-called accidents happened to anyone considered to be an Enemy of the State.

He embarked for England in haste the following day, taking his foreign currency, mostly in dollars, with him. He left enough Deutschmarks in Alice's bank account to cover the upkeep of their home and feed the family.

* * *

Back in his home town he booked into a hotel near Marble Arch. He chose an expensive suite; in Berlin he had acquired a taste for luxurious living and spent money as if there were no tomorrow. He was an easy touch for every one of his *émigré* friends who had also sought sanctuary in England.

Alice sold the apartment's expensive furniture and other valuable objects to raise money to rent temporary furnished accommodation for her parents and sister before joining her husband in London with her son.

Felix awaited his family's arrival at the Channel port full of joy. He praised his wife for her judicious business acumen, something he completely lacked. He insisted on travelling first class back to London so that they could enjoy their reunion in style. Alice raised an eyebrow, but was too happy to object.

A scent of fresh, red roses greeted her in every room when they entered the suite. Excited and exuberant, her husband led her through the three exquisitely furnished rooms, expecting his wife's approval.

She was horrified at his extravagance.

"How long do you think your dollars will last?"

"You only deserve the very best. I've put my feelers out

to raise money for the type of revue I co-produced in Berlin. I have not been idle!"

Alice did not comment.

"Quite a few Jewish artists are in London. With local talent for the chorus line, I should get a show together to be staged at the Embassy Theatre in Swiss Cottage, North West London, where many refugees are living, as well as filing copy to the press."

"Your contract with the paper as a foreign correspondent has ended, now that you are here, not in Berlin. And how can we get by in the meantime?"

He had no answer.

Next day, early in the morning, she set off with him in tow to find cheaper accommodation. For convenience sake, he wanted to be near the theatre. They alighted from the Bakerloo Line underground at West Hampstead Station and looked at the 'flats to let' in the estate agent's window near the exit. They needed a home for the three of them and eventually Alice's family, including her brother's half-Jewish son whose parents worried about his future if he remained with them in Germany.

Alice, purposeful and practical, decided not to waste any time. She led her perplexed husband into the agency and, with next to no English at her command, explained they wanted to view one of the flats which happened to be within five minutes walk, opposite the synagogue. Felix followed them meekly as they went up the stairs and through the entrance door into the sparsely furnished three rooms, kitchen and outmoded bathroom.

With a nod, his wife indicated this would do. A contract was drawn up back in the office. The family moved in a week later. It was very difficult for Felix to disguise his sorrow that they should have sunk so low. Yet, he was certain that their luck would turn again soon.

* * *

Alice's sister had wisely enrolled in a dressmaking course, showing an unexpected flair for dress design. As soon as she had arrived with her parents, the sisters went to the refugee committee, then in Bloomsbury House in London, to ask for help. The volunteer adviser, impressed by the two women who wore dresses designed and sewn by hand, procured for them a second-hand sewing machine and the loan of sufficient funds to get them started.

"I am going to be your first client. If you can make up a dress for me, suitable to wear in the office, I will recommend you to the other ladies in the building. No doubt, you will also be able to do alterations."

Within a week the sewing machine was delivered. After the pattern and material had been handed over by their first client, they started to work straight away. Betty was in charge, while Alice with her agile fingers became her assistant.

Full of anxiety they returned with the dress. Her customer was delighted with it, put it on and paraded in it through the other offices. Many orders followed, enough to pay for the household expenses and to feed seven members of their family, including two teenagers whose appetites were enormous.

But conditions in the flat were too cramped for such a large family. The dressmaking business had to be carried out in Betty's small room, a clothes line attached between two walls for their clients' garments. They worked all day until late at night. Another solution had to be found to make ends meet, and at the same time be a more comfortable home for the three generations of their family.

Felix felt completely hemmed in by the lack of space, surrounded by all his wife's relations. He made the rounds of Fleet Street in an effort to obtain at least some freelance work. No one seemed to have time to spare for him. He was still trapped in the life he had left behind in Berlin. In his absence of twenty-seven years too much had changed socially and politically for him to catch up. He was out of touch with the mood and aspirations of the readership. His prose was outdated: it had not sufficiently kept pace with new idioms and phrases which had enriched the English language while he was abroad. Even the articles he submitted to broadsheet editors about the annexation of the Sudetenland, the part of Czechoslovakia populated mainly by Germans, or Hitler's negation of the Munich Agreement with Neville Chamberlain in 1938, were not accepted.

Always an optimist (he still had some money at his disposal), he shrugged off what was, after all, just a setback, and considered it a good omen. He decided to produce a cabaret with many of the talented Jewish artists, such as the actor Anton Walbrück, the singer Richard Tauber, the cartoonist Vicky, (including choreographers and composers who were now in this country. (I found a copy of the programme with these illustrious names among my late husband's possessions.) His enthusiasm was such that he convinced his family to go along with him. With the generous patronage of a well-heeled theatrical refugee and English backers he raised enough money. As in Berlin, he found a cafe where he was allowed to sit at a corner table to write the material for a show while consuming many cups of black coffee.

The Embassy Theatre, now a drama school with the modern Hampstead Theatre on the opposite side of the road, was situated in the heart of North West London, the new 'fiefdom' that the Continental refugees had made their own.

Once the English dancers had been rehearsed to perfection, he invited the press for the dress rehearsal. The reporters, in a consensus of opinion, rated the revue as one of the best seen in the capital for years.

But the show was a complete flop. Central Europeans immigrants, who wanted to forget their present woes while reliving past happy days with their friends, came to see the performance, but this type of continental entertainment did not appeal to the general public. It was too sophisticated for the man in the street, unlike the productions in music halls. It closed down after a week.

Felix had pinned all his hopes on it, though Alice had expressed her doubts right from the start. As usual, he paid no heed to her misgivings and had pursued his plans whatever the outcome.

He was still resilient, not yet beaten. Motivated by the will to succeed in order to offer his family the kind of existence they had enjoyed before, he intended to write a witness account of life in 'The Twenties in Berlin', valuable resource material for students of recent history, with the certainty that the manuscript would be accepted by one of the refugee publishers, André Deutsch or Paul Hamlyn. Even Alice gave her blessing, although she doubted that it would bring in the royalties her husband had predicted.

It did not happen. Being so pre-occupied by the

framework of the book, he stumbled on a curb in the street and fell while he was out shopping for the household. An ambulance took him to the hospital. His wife was alerted. He was slightly concussed. Before discharging him, the doctor in the emergency ward assured them that he had had a lucky escape. But the after effects were disastrous.

His loved ones witnessed the daily change which came over him, as his powers of concentration decreased. However much he tried, he was unable to recapture the technique of putting ideas into flowing, meaningful prose on paper. Thoroughly discouraged, he gave up, resigned to his fate.

The two industrious sisters had by then saved enough money for the new venture to materialize; to rent (if possible buy at a later stage), one of the large detached Victorian houses off Quex Road, near West Hampstead Underground Station, she had inspected from the outside. She wanted to turn it into a boarding house for elderly refugees who yearned to be in a Continental environment where German was spoken. At their advanced age, it was proving extremely difficult to adjust in a foreign country.

The house belonged to a serving member of the Armed Forces whose American wife had returned to her family for the duration of the war. An estate agent had been charged to put the furniture into storage and let it to responsible people who would appreciate the stained glass windows of the front door, the high ceiling ground floor rooms with central heating half way up the property.

Again, escorted by Felix, as her knowledge of English had not improved, she signed the lease. They moved in on Battle of Britain Day with essential pieces of furniture they had gradually acquired. The family occupied three of the eight rooms; the sister sharing one with their mother on the first floor; the boys in a small room half way up the stairs towards the top floor where Alice and Felix slept. There was never mention of Abraham. He must have passed away.

With a loan from their local butcher (moved by the two women's fortitude), they managed to furnish one first floor room and let it to a middle-aged, slightly mentally disturbed Jewish woman. She had been introduced to them by one of the welfare workers of a Jewish organisation.

Her family was so pleased a home with compassionate people had been found for her, that they paid double the monthly rent. This allowed the sisters get two more rooms ready for refugee senior citizens. As their income increased, all rooms were fitted out for occupation and let. The sisters' hospitality and the excellent cuisine increased their reputation in the Jewish community, so much so that there was second sitting: hot lunches and dinners for half-a-dozen local residents who were too old to cook hot meals without help.

By the time I first stepped over the threshold into the kitchen, a waiting list was pinned to one of the walls. The house had been bought a few months earlier.

Felix, always smiling when out and about, had noticed a 'To Let' sign outside the property next door. His wife felt confident enough to find boarders for the additional rooms. A cook, always closely watched by Alice, was employed. The married couple was housed next door. The wife cleaned the rooms, the husband served the meals and acted as a general handyman. Two part-time women had been hired. It was a flourishing business.

Felix acted as an interpreter when his wife had to deal with solicitors, estate agents and official agencies. But he was always in the shadows. He never tired of undertaking menial tasks in the household in multiple ways, such as stoking the fire in the large oven in the kitchen and carrying coal from a small shed next to the building during the couple's day off.

Neither Alice, nor her son volunteered to tell me how he must have felt during those last years. He may have been relieved he was of some use to his wife. It is also possible that he might have lost his self-esteem.

He died of angina pectoris according the death certificate. No one ever told me whether he became bedridden, passed away suddenly at home, or whether his life ended in a hospital bed.

Alice never mentioned his last days during the many years I knew her. It seemed to me that she wanted to remember their heydays together and obliterate the memory of his declining intellect.

Made in the USA
Charleston, SC
19 February 2016